KING
AMONG THE
THEOLOGIANS

THEOLOGIANS

NOEL LEO ERSKINE
FOREWORD BY BERNICE A. KING

The Pilgrim Press
Cleveland, Ohio

The Pilgrim Press, Cleveland, Ohio 44115
© 1994 by Noel Leo Erskine

Foreword © 1994 by Bernice A. King

99 98 97 96 95   5 4 3 2

Library of Congress Cataloging-in-Publication Data

Erskine, Noel Leo.
King among the theologians / Noel Leo Erskine ;
foreword by Bernice A. King.
p.   cm.
Includes bibliographical references and index.
ISBN 0-8298-1015-3
1. Black theology.   2. Theology—History—20th century.
3. King, Martin Luther, Jr., 1929–1968.   I. Title.
BT82.7.E77   1994   230'.61'092—dc20
94-23380   CIP

*For my
children
Donna
June
Leo
And my
mother
Lynda Erskine*

CONTENTS

FOREWORD

Since the untimely death of my father, Martin Luther King Jr., there has been much focus on his contributions to civil and human rights. Much of the emphasis has surrounded his activist spirit in the struggle for freedom, justice, and equality for oppressed people. However, if one were to do a complete study of the life of my father, one would discover that he was more than a "civil rights leader."

As one who matriculated through theology schools where I studied the great theologians, I strongly support Dr. Erskine's supposition that my father is a theologian in his own right. The greatest support for this is that daddy understood and interpreted most events of his life in the context of the divine. His life was a walking sermon inspired by God. He not only practiced what he preached, but he preached what he practiced. Upon observing the life and leadership of my father, you would readily see the emergence of the Holy Scriptures. In fact, many of the great Christian doctrines can be seen emanating from the movement he led. In particular, it was the doctrine of reconciliation that gave meaning and purpose to the nonviolent philosophy that defined this movement.

In his book *Stride Toward Freedom* my father stated that "today the choice is no longer between violence and nonviolence. The choice is either nonviolence or nonexistence."[1] The central theme of my father's philosophy of life comes from this statement. For him, to be Christian means to be totally committed to the "love ethic" of Jesus Christ. If this love manifests itself in its highest form (i.e., agape) then the only route that an individual can follow is a total commitment to the nonviolent way of life. The other alternative is destruction.

It is common knowledge that the opposite of destruction is creation. As such, it is the creation of the "beloved community" that my father worked to attain. For him, nonviolence was the means for creating this community. Inherent in this process is reconciliation, which is the bringing together of estranged forces. Therefore, reconciliation becomes the act of creating community, which is only possible through love and nonviolence. This is certainly consistent with the theological understanding that "God so loved the world" that through the person of Jesus Christ God entered into the brokenness of humanity and restored it by way of the redeeming act on the cross.

Further discussion of my father and the doctrine of reconciliation is in the following pages. Surrounding and supporting this discussion, Dr. Erskine makes a case for my father as a theologian through dialogue with four theological perspectives.

I cannot adequately express in words how elated I am that *King Among the Theologians* has been written. It puts my father in a category that he is most deserving of. As my father used to eloquently state, "Truth crushed to the earth shall rise again." Dr. Erskine has put forth a long-awaited truth. Those whose criticisms have sought to undermine and destroy my father's place in history will have to revisit their claims on coming across this scholarly work.

King Among the Theologians I hope is only the beginning of a new frontier of scholarly research concerning the life and thought of Dr. Martin Luther King Jr. If it continues, generations yet unborn will perhaps appreciate and understand more fully the true essence of Martin Luther King Jr. If not, our children and our children's children will be the beneficiaries of inferior research. This could lead them to revere him as merely a historical figure whose contributions have no relevance to their present-day reality. How tragic this would be. After all, as a theologian and a prophet, the contributions of my father are timeless because "God is the same yesterday, today, and tomorrow."

BERNICE A. KING

PREFACE

Studies on the life and thought of Martin Luther King Jr. have explored King's role as a civil rights activist or presented him as a philosopher who synthesized the views of others. What is surprising is that although King's doctorate at Boston University was in systematic theology, and Black theology emerged as part of his theological legacy, the interpreters of King's thought have not in any sustained way explored King's contribution as a theologian.

This work sets out to investigate King's contribution as a theologian, locating the primary context of his work in the Black church. Whenever the question "What is theology?" is raised, we tend to turn to traditional models for an answer, therefore I propose to look at four approaches to the theological task and place each in conversation with King.

I will examine the theological approaches of Paul Tillich, Karl Barth, James Cone, and that of womanist theology, reflected in the work of Katie Cannon and Jacquelyn Grant, with the intention of forging a dialogue with King's theological perspective.

Tillich's work is significant because King's dissertation for Boston University examined Tillich's understanding of God. Further, during the civil rights movement, King would often turn to Tillich's work for spiritual and theological sustenance as he became weary in the struggle.

Karl Barth's approach to theology will also be examined not only because he had a profound effect on liberation theology in general and Black theology in particular but also because King was familiar with his work and wrote articles and term papers on Barth's doctrine of God. During Barth's visit to the United

States in 1963, he and King were able to meet. (It is regrettable that although Tillich and King lived in the same country they never met.)

Cone's approach to theology is examined because Cone and King are sons of the Black church. Cone draws heavily from King's work, especially as Cone articulates his understanding of ontological blackness, God of the oppressed and the community of the oppressed. It goes without saying, however, that King would have problems with the concepts *Black power, Black theology,* and *God is black.* Chapter 5, which explores King's theology, asks what King's theological contribution would look like if King had had the benefit of a dialogue with Cone's approach to theology.

Finally, King's work is placed in conversation with womanist theology as it is represented by Jacquelyn Grant and Katie Cannon. Chapter 6 serves as an internal critique of King's work and the Black church, in that womanist theology helps expose the myopic tendency in both King's work and the Black church to exclude women from leadership roles and responsibilities. It also points to the roots of the beloved community.

What all these theological perspectives have in common is the passion for reuniting the alienated and the estranged. But King goes a step further. He models for us the marks of the theologian:

1. The theologian must work from within the struggle to relate Christian faith to the concrete conditions that affect both body and soul.

2. The theologian must be committed to the struggle to change the world as well as willing to lay down his or her life in the quest for justice for the oppressed. This means that the concrete problems of the community must become grist for the theological mill. Issues of economic, social, and political justice, poverty, and powerlessness must be brought from the periphery to the center of theological attention.

3. Reconciliation becomes the main key in which theology is set.

4. Faith and praxis are conjoined as the gospel of Jesus is related to the plight of those who suffer and are heavy laden.

These are the marks of the theologian, and these are the marks of Martin Luther King Jr.'s legacy—a legacy that continues to challenge the shape of the church and society.

ACKNOWLEDGMENTS

This work would not have reached its final stage without the help I received from many persons and institutions. Its first impulse was formed in a team-taught course with Coretta Scott King at Emory University during several semesters. To the many students who contributed to this course I am most grateful. A sabbatical at the Methodist Training Institute, in Meru, Kenya, provided most useful space and time for dialogue with faculty and students. To colleagues and friends who read all or parts of this work I am most grateful. I am especially indebted to Jacquelyn Grant, Pamela Couture, Robert Franklin, Theodore Runyon, Alvin Brown, Flora Bridges, Thomas Thangaraj, James Fowler, and my mentor and friend, James Cone. A special word of appreciation to my editor, Richard Brown, for his patience and gentle prodding. Without the sacrifice of my wife, Glenda, and our family, the completion of this project would not have been possible. As in all things I am most grateful to them.

CHAPTER 1

THE BLACK CHURCH AND KING'S THEOLOGY

Almost five years after the death of Dr. Martin Luther King Jr., an editorial that appeared in *Christian Century* (January 1973) examined "King's continuing impact" and pronounced his enormous influence on America—an influence that extended to the White House and through presidents Kennedy and Johnson.[1] King was in fact extolled as a social activist who had made an enduring contribution to the world. One of his chief gifts was that of moving people with the power and clarity of his rhetoric. The editorial remarks, "[A] rereading of King's *Where Do We Go From Here? Chaos or Community* reminds us that he recognized in 1967 that the civil rights movement needed to move into economic and political arenas—and even into the international struggle for human rights. The book ought to be required reading for every rights activist of our nation."[2]

Although this assessment of King broke new ground in suggesting that he envisioned economic and political reform as the basis for the new America, it nonetheless failed to acknowledge the significance of King as a *theologian*. The perception of his legacy extended only to his work as an activist and visionary who influenced the social and political history of the United States. In spite of his significant contribution to the development of Black theology, there was not a hint in the editorial that King had left any theological legacy at all.

1

One of the first to acknowledge King as a theologian was Herbert Richardson. In his article "Martin Luther King—Unsung Theologian" he made the bold claim that indeed King was the most important theologian of his time. With unprecedented clarity King had given great care and thought to the problem of evil and especially to the ways in which structures of evil oppress people. Richardson writes:

> King's perception of the human problem today as rooted in a certain structure of social evil led him to emphasize again and again that his struggle was directed against the forces, or structure, of evil itself rather than against the person or group who is doing the evil. Christian faith sees neither particular men nor particular groups as evil, but sees them trapped within a structure of ideological separation which makes ritual conflict inevitable. In order to overcome this kind of evil, faith does not attack the men who do evil, but the structure of evil which makes men act violently.[3]

This understanding of evil, argues Richardson, gives King's theology a critical focus that is duplicated nowhere else in contemporary thought. Furthermore, this understanding of faith's role in a world of evil allowed King to become the proponent of a theology of reconciliation.

Professor James Earl Massey shares the perspective of Dr. Richardson, reminding us that King was trained as a systematic theologian and articulated a theology that was radical, relevant, and redemptive. King sought to give theology a human shape and place it at the service of the human community. Massey codifies the main tenets of King's theology:

> King believed and taught that the life and teachings of Jesus are not just radical but relevant and redemptive. He was convinced that life at its source and center is personal, and that every person has inherent worth, so he dedicated himself to serve the needs of persons, and to do that service

in the spirit of trust and love—thus, his prolonged and
persistent push for needed social change, and for just laws
to replace the unjust strictures by which black life had been
shackled.[4]

James Cone, one of the ablest exponents of Black theology, refers to Martin King's teachings as fundamental to the development of Black theology and calls on Black theologians to build on the base King has established.[5] More recently, Cone has acknowledged King as a theologian who worked within the tradition of the Black church.[6] Agreeing with Cone that we must locate the true sources of King's theology in this milieu, James Evans writes:

Most intellectual treatments of King's thought focus
on the influence which white thinkers had on him, but
neglect the impact of the most important formative factor
in his life, the Afro-American Baptist Church. Liberal
theology failed him. Gandhi's non-violent method had been
confined to personal relations and was incapable, without
modification, of addressing the structural misuse of power;
Thoreau's civil disobedience only worked in a situation of
moral and political equality, which did not exist between
white Americans and Afro-Americans. The bedrock of King's
theology was not laid at Crozer Theological Seminary or at
Boston University, but in the Afro-American Baptist Church
of his youth, and at Morehouse College . . . King's dream
grew out of the spirituality of the Afro-American tradition.[7]

Whereas Professor Evans does not deny the role of white sources in King's theology, he is careful to assert that the wellspring of King's theology—and the key to comprehending it fully—must be sought within the Black church. Evans, like Cone, argues that although King would appeal to white intellectual sources to provide the framework for his discourses on love, nonviolence and the relationship of the gospel of Jesus to the plight of the poor, it is quite clear that his work is anchored in the Black tradition. His call to serve the leadership of the Southern Christian Leadership Conference (SCLC) was made in the context of the Black church, and a great deal of his support came from there. Furthermore, his position as co-pastor of Ebenezer Baptist Church while he served as president of SCLC points to an intention to keep his commitment and identification with the Black church intact. Cone states succinctly: "King's close ties with the Black Church, in preference over the alternatives, indicates that his primary commitment was to that community. Anyone, therefore, who wishes to understand his life and thought must make the Black Church the primary source for the analysis."[8]

We must now examine the claim so firmly articulated by Evans and Cone that it is the Black church, and not white intellectual sources, that stands as the foundation of the theology of Martin Luther King Jr. In his groundbreaking work *The Negro Church in America,* E. Franklin Frazier identifies five critical roles the Black church served in the Black community. He points out that since slavery destroyed the Black family, one of the tasks assumed by the Black church was to restore it. Furthermore, because the plantation destroyed organized social life and conventions of moral and sexual behavior, it was up to the Black church to restructure and organize Black communal life. The Black church also provided leadership in the area of civic and legal responsibilities as these impinged on communal and family life.

It is no secret that the Black community has turned to the Black church not only for the spiritual sustenance of its hymns and prayers but also for the social and political support of leadership and direction. The Black church certainly proved to be a primary organizational resource in 1955, when Mrs. Rosa Parks refused to relinquish her seat in the front of a bus in Montgomery, Alabama. Confronting the victimization of a Black family member and the need of a Black community for unifying leadership, Martin King was able to fill the breach with the help of the Black church. It was not his reading of the writings of the social gospel theologian Walter Rauschenbusch that provided the basis for his understanding that the task of the

Black church was to redeem the soul of the community—in fact, it was his life in the community, as well as the demands the community made on the church, that made this obvious. The Black church's efforts to take the teachings of Jesus seriously made it imperative that the church reach out and redeem the soul of all of America. King puts it this way:

> From the beginning a basic philosophy guided the movement. This guiding principle has been referred to variously as nonviolent resistance, noncooperation, and passive resistance. But in the first days of the protest none of these expressions was mentioned; the phrase most often heard was "Christian love." It was the Sermon on the Mount, rather than a doctrine of passive resistance, that initially inspired the Negroes of Montgomery to dignified social action. It was Jesus of Nazareth that stirred the Negroes to protest with the creative weapon of love.[9]

In addition to providing organizational leadership in the Black community, the Black church is also credited by Frazier with providing the Black community with economic leadership. The Black community has become accustomed to providing meager resources to purchase land and materials to build its churches. In the time of Richard Allen and Absalom Jones, for example, the Black church in Philadelphia promoted the organization of sickness and burial societies to provide support for dependents in times of catastrophic illness or death of the household breadwinner. Later the Black church organized credit unions and benevolent societies to provide for the community's day-to-day financial needs. There were even some congregations that began their association as benevolent societies whose affiliative purpose was sustaining people materially as well as spiritually.

Being true to the Black church tradition, King removes issues of economics from the periphery and brings them to the center of theological attention. Christianity is thus not only a creed but also a protest struggle against poverty and oppression. In his essay "Pilgrimage to Nonviolence," King writes:

> The Christian ought always to be challenged by any protest against unfair treatment of the poor, for Christianity is itself such a protest, nowhere expressed more eloquently than in Jesus' words: "The Spirit of the Lord is upon me, because he hath anointed me to preach the gospel to the poor; he hath sent me to heal the broken hearted, to preach deliverance to captives, and recovering of sight to the blind, to set at liberty them that are bruised, to preach the acceptable year of the Lord." [10]

In the last three years of his life, economic issues became a central theme in King's speeches and writings. He was increasingly troubled by the gap between rich and poor, as well as the separation of white and black. In what is perhaps his most radical speech he talks about divine dissatisfaction becoming a basis for activism and progress:

> Let us go out with a "divine dissatisfaction." . . . Let us be dissatisfied until the tragic walls that separate the outer city of wealth and comfort and the inner city of poverty and despair shall be crushed by the battering rams of the forces of justice. Let us be dissatisfied until those that live on the outskirts of hope are brought into the metropolis of daily security. Let us be dissatisfied until slums are cast into the junk heaps of history, and every family is living in a decent sanitary home. [11]

King learned about this divine dissatisfaction in the Black church. He did not have to wait to read Rauschenbusch at Crozer Seminary to be introduced to the church's responsibility in the area of economics. Perhaps the reason he liked Rauschenbusch was that his theology reaffirmed the historical convictions of the Black church.

Another role of the Black church that Frazier identifies is its organization of political power for the masses. In a world in which

Black people had limited political power, the Black church became *the* political arena for Black people. Frazier describes the church's involvement:

> *The Negro Church was not only an arena of political life for the leaders of the Negroes, it has a political meaning for the masses. Although they were denied the right to vote in the American community, within their churches, especially the Methodist churches, they could vote and engage in electing their own officers. The elections of Bishops and other officers and representatives to conventions has been a serious activity for the masses of Negroes. But, in addition, the church had a political significance for the Negroes in a broader meaning of the term. The development of the Negro church after emancipation was tied up, as we have seen, largely with the Negro family.*[12]

King concentrated his energies and commitment on those who were excluded from economic and political power. King did not use the Black church as a base for political power to gain elective office. Rather, he used the power base of the Black church to secure human and civil rights for the masses. He frequently cited the joyful exclamation of a bystander who learned that the United States Supreme Court had ruled that Alabama's state and local bus segregation laws were unconstitutional: "God Almighty has spoken from Washington!"[13]

There was a theological commitment from Martin King to work on justice for those forced onto the margins of society, and he believed that God was involved in this task.

The Black church also played a vital role in providing education for the Black community. According to Frazier, the Black church sought to meet this critical need by building the surest pathway out of economic and social marginalization into the American mainstream. Concerning the Black churches' investment in education, Lawrence Jones writes:

The churches' historic concern for education initially focussed on efforts to compensate for the exclusion of Blacks from access to elementary education. After emancipation, the most pressing concern became that of establishing and supporting secondary schools and colleges. By 1900 the churches had compiled an impressive record; Black Baptist associations were supporting some 80 elementary schools and 18 academies and colleges; the African Methodist Episcopal Churches were underwriting 32 secondary and collegiate institutions; and the smaller AME Zion denomination was supporting eight. The denomination now named the Christian Methodist Episcopal church, only 30 years old in 1900, had established five schools.[14]

Martin King appealed constantly for school integration as a part of his vision for the "beloved community." His own life was a testimony to the importance he attached to education and his commitment to education dedicated to the service of God and the community. When he became pastor of Dexter Avenue Baptist Church, one of his first tasks was to form a committee to raise money to help a Dexter High School graduate earn a college degree.

Lastly, Frazier contends that the Black church provided a refuge for the Black community in a hostile white world. Although Black people were denied participation in the social and economic life of mainstream America and were not accepted in white institutions of higher education, the church provided a creative context in which political power and justice were the right of the community. It was the theological commitments to justice, love, and the empowerment of the oppressed that uniquely equipped the Black church to become the base camp of the Black community in the long march to freedom and equality. The only institution that could give birth to and sustain the civil rights movement was the Black church. Often before people went out to face beatings and police-dog attacks from so-called law enforcement officials, they entered the sanctuary of the Black church to pray. The church became not only the symbol of hope but the agent of reconciliation for the Black community. Here in the refuge of the church, Martin King would inform the weary travelers that Almighty God was committed to their struggle and victory was assured if they would but endure to the end.

Martin King was a son of the Black church, and his theology cannot be understood without referring to those origins. Because his social activism was based on theological convictions about God and humanity, he gave particular attention to an explication of Christian faith in a situation of oppression. Faith for him was the victorious struggle against injustice and oppression of all sorts. Faith as the power of reconciliation becomes faithfulness to God as one lives out one's commitment for a restored and reconciled community. Faith in the mission to create the reconciled and restored community becomes the goal of history.

The moral task of the theologian then becomes the proclamation of the dominion of God and the struggle in history to make God's dominion a present reality. The central task of the theologian is not so much the arbitration between theology and philosophy as an assessment of what must be done in history to effect the restored and reconciled community. King's understanding of God required changes in the foundation of society in order that God's children may be free. Therefore, to know God is to become impatient with an order that denies God's children their God-given rights. Faith in God also means breaking laws that conflict with the eternal law of God. Raising the practical issue of how one distinguishes between a just and an unjust law, King writes:

> A just law is a man made code that squares with the moral law or the law of God. An unjust law is a code that is out of harmony with the moral law. To put it in terms of St. Thomas Aquinas: An unjust law is a human law that is not rooted in eternal law and natural law. Any law that uplifts human personality is just. Any law that degrades human personality is unjust. All segregation statues are unjust because segregation distorts the soul and damages the personality. . . . Segregation, to use the terminology of the

Jewish philosopher Martin Buber, substitutes an "I-it" relationship for an "I-thou" relationship and ends up relegating persons to the status of things. . . . Paul Tillich has said that sin is separation. Is not segregation an existential expression of man's tragic separation, his awful estrangement, his terrible sinfulness?[15]

In fleshing out his understanding of faith as commitment to make the world human, King gives sociological concreteness to Buber's "I-thou" relationship, St. Thomas Aquinas's understanding of the eternal law, and Tillich's understanding of sin as existential estrangement. It is to Tillich's thought and its relationship to King's theology that we now turn.

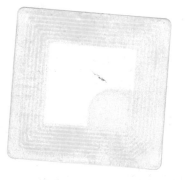

CHAPTER 2 PAUL TILLICH'S PERSPECTIVE

Tillich makes it quite clear that the task of theology is to make manifest in the message of the gospel the answer to the existential questions posed by human existence. In Tillich's formulation, theology comes to life between the poles of the situational and the confessional, and it attempts, however tentatively, to correlate the human question with the divine answer. Tillich argues with good effect that human reason experiences a "fall," just as every other aspect of life does, from an essential to an existential state. Human reason, therefore, needs salvation, and reason's salvation is by means of revelation.

As Tillich sets forth this discussion, he talks about three stages in the life and development of reason: the structure and function of human reason in its essential state, the various conflicts that reason endures in its existential state, and the reintegration of reason as the ultimate end.

Tillich emphasizes that he is not overly concerned with technical reason, which he calls *reasoning,* or the capacity for analytical or systematic thought. This is the reason with which students are concerned in a classroom setting. The student needs to be reminded, however, that theology is not afraid of technical reason, but it is deeply conscious of reason's limits.

The primary task of technical reason is to assist and support the fundamental category of ontological reason. Tillich speaks of *ontological reason* as that structure of the mind that allows it to grasp and shape reality. This definition of ontological reason enables Tillich to highlight both its subjective and objective character. Subjective reason points to that quality of the mind that allows it to grasp and shape reality. Objective reason is the rational structure of reality that can be grasped and shaped. Subjective reason has a "receptive" relation to the world that it grasps and shapes. It grasps by understanding a thing or event or other selves. It shapes by transforming reality.

Here Tillich hints at the correspondence between subjective reason of the mind and the objective reason in the universe. According to Tillich, reason in both its subjective and objective forms points to its depth. In spite of the fallen nature of reason, all rational functions point beyond themselves to the ultimate and are transparent to it.

The depth of reason that points reason beyond reason is seen most clearly in the rational functions of myth and cult. Myth is not primitive science, nor is cult primitive morality. Rather these two manifestations of reason indicate that even under the conditions of actual existence, even in its fallen state, reason has within it a depth and power that points beyond itself to truth itself, beauty itself, justice itself, or love itself.

But existential reason knows finiteness, ambiguities, and self-destructive conflict. The major conflicts as Tillich sees them are between autonomy and heteronomy, absolutism and relativism, and formalism and emotionalism. The good news, however, is that existential reason, in spite of existential estrangement and its destructive conflicts, is not without the infinite. In the real world its basic structure is never lost. In spite of the alienation and estrangement that befall reason, it is never without its depth. This is what provides hope for fallen reason and offers to reason the possibility of revelation. In the conflict between absolutism and relativism, reason asks for that which can unite the relative and the absolute: "Only that which is absolute and relative at the same time can over come this conflict. Only revelation can do it."[1] Reason does not resist revelation, for revelation means the reintegration of reason.

According to Tillich, if reason raises the question, then revelation provides the answer. If faith is the state of being ultimately concerned, revelation is the manifestation of what concerns us ultimately. Revelation is the manifestation of the "mystery" of the ground of our being. But revelation is rather similar to reason in that it also has two parts. It has an objective and a subjective side. For Tillich there can be no revelation without someone to receive it. The subjective aspect is the receiving side of it. Revelation is received through the ecstasy of the mind. The objective aspect is the revelatory act wherein the mystery takes hold of the subject through miracle.

A *mystery* is something that is essentially hidden and cannot lose its mysteriousness when revealed. True mystery appears when mystery is driven beyond itself. Thus mystery is the ground of being; it is being itself. Whenever the ultimate question, "What does it mean to be?" is posed, by implication there is something, and there is also the possibility that there can be nothing. So on the negative side there is a certain kind of shock that grips the mind when it faces the threat of nonbeing, the abyss, in everything. On the positive side the mystery appears as the power of being, conquering nonbeing. It appears as our ultimate concern.

On the other hand, *ecstasy* means to stand outside oneself. In the ecstatic state the mind transcends the ordinary situation. Ecstasy is the state of mind in which reason is beyond itself, beyond its subject/object structure. If revelation is the showing forth of what concerns us ultimately, and if it occurs as the mind is grasped by the *mysterium tremendum,* and if it is received in a condition of ecstasy when reason is elevated beyond itself, then God is not perceived in the ordinary forms of knowledge, and revelation must not be thought of as divinely imparted teachings, doctrines, or information about the world and the events of history.

A *miracle,* or *sign-event,* is an occurrence that astounds us and conveys to us the mystery of being. A genuine miracle does not destroy the structure of reality any more than ecstasy destroys or contradicts the structure of the mind. A miracle must be received as a sign-event in an ecstatic experience. The marks of a revelatory experience are mystery, ecstasy, and miracle. For revelation to take place, there must be a correlation between mystery and ecstasy. In Jesus Christ, who is the final and unsurpassable revelation, a correlation of ecstasy and miracle takes place. He is the miracle of the final revelation and completely demonstrates in his being the mystery of the ground of being, and his reception is the final revelation.

Further, Tillich states that questions raised about reason are correlated with the answers of revelation:

> *The method of correlation explains the contents of the Christian faith through existential questions and theological answers in mutual interdependence. . . . Theology formulates the questions implied in human existence, and theology formulates the answers implied in divine self-manifestation under the guidance of the questions implied in human existence. This is a circle which drives man to a point where question and answer are not separated. This point, however, is not a moment in time. It belongs to man's essential being, to the unity of his finitude with the infinity in which he was created and from which he is separated.*[2]

The theologian has two primary tasks. The first task is to be a philosopher and analyze the existential situation. Although the theologian will correlate findings with theological insights, the theologian works as a philosopher, investigating the cultural forms that express human existence. The theologian works as a philosopher fixing the eyes on Christian symbols that point to the answer. If something arises out of human existence that is unexpected in light of the theological answer, the answer must be "reformulated."

The second task of the theologian is to make plain that the Christian message truly supplies the answers to the questions implied in human existence. Theology supplies the answers from the sources (the Bible, church history, the history of religion and culture), through the medium (participatory experience), and under the norm (the New Being in Jesus as the Christ is our ultimate concern).

CONCERNING METHOD

Tillich speaks of his method as that of correlation. Theology correlates existential questions with our ultimate concern. We could also speak of Tillich's approach to theology as covenantal—a theology in which the partnership between God and humanity is evident. The divine–human encounter means for Tillich that human beings raise the question, and God provides the answer; it is sometimes under the impact of the divine answer that human beings ask the question. There is a mutual dependence of "God for us" and "we for God." The term *ultimate concern* points to this encounter with the religious in which all reality participates. Tillich points out the different approaches of the philosopher of religion and the theologian to this "ultimate concern":

> *The ultimate concern or the religious encounter with*
> *reality can be considered in two ways. It can be looked at as*
> *an event beside other events, to be observed and described*
> *in theoretical detachment, or it can be understood as an*
> *event in which he who considers it is "existentially"*
> *involved. In the first case the philosopher of religion is at*
> *work, in the second the theologian speaks. The philosopher*
> *of religion notices the ultimate concern, which he cannot*
> *help finding in the history of religion as a quality of*
> *practically all representative personalities, symbols and*
> *activities, that are called "religious." But in his dealing with*
> *this characteristic of religion he himself is only theoretically*
> *but not existentially concerned. The religious concern is not*
> *his concern insofar as he is a philosopher of religion. He*
> *points to it, he explains it but his work is not an expression*
> *of the religious encounter with reality. This is different with*
> *the theologian. He applies his ultimate concern to*
> *everything, as an* ultimate *concern demands—even to his*
> *theoretical interpretation of the religious encounter. For the*

*theologian the interpretation of the ultimate concern is itself
a matter of ultimate concern, a religious work.*[3]

Tillich goes on to contend that the philosopher cannot escape a
religious background nor can the theologian avoid a philosophical
tool. Further, he adds, "No theologian should be taken seriously as a
theologian, even if he is a great Christian and a great scholar, if his
work shows that he does not take philosophy seriously."[4]

Tillich reminds us that there are two formal criteria for every
theology: (a) The object of theology is what concerns us ultimately:
only those propositions that deal with their object insofar as It can
become a matter of ultimate concern for us are theological; and (b)
only those statements that deal with their object insofar as it can
become a matter of being or not being for us are theological. The
importance of the first criterion is that it helps us to distinguish
between ultimate concerns and preliminary concerns. This criterion
protects the theologian from the danger of confusing theological
statements with scientific, historical, political, or other questions
that focus our relation with the world of existence: "Those propositions are theological which deal with a subject insofar as it belongs
to the foundation of our being and insofar as the meaning of our
existence depends upon it."[5]

This approach protects the Protestant principle of not elevating
the relative to the realm of the absolute. The second criterion
sharpens for us Tillich's existentialist approach to theology. It is this
approach that determines his method, that of seeking in the Christian
message answers to the existential questions raised by the situation.
It is here that the ultimate concern expresses itself in the actualities
of life, embodied in our symbols and our actions.

METHOD IN REGARD TO THE BIBLE AND TRADITION

Tillich affirms the Bible as the theologian's primary source.
The Bible is primary for the theologian for three reasons. First, it is
the record of the decisive manifestation of what concerns us ultimately, in the picture of Jesus as the Christ. This is the standard by

which all Christian theology is measured, "the criterion also of the theological use of the Bible." Second, the Bible presents us with the original witnesses who were instrumental in the formation of the early church. Each biblical writer is a witness to the new reality manifested in Jesus as the Christ. Tillich points out that in a profound sense we could say that these writers started the tradition. These writers call attention to the one who judges the tradition, including their own contribution to it. Because of this, the Bible is not of itself the standard by which Christian theology is judged. The Bible becomes normative as it witnesses to the new reality. A primary task of Christian theology is to identify the norm of Christian theology as this emerges from the biblical text and tradition.

The third element of the Bible's importance is general revelation. If Jesus the Christ constitutes special revelation, Tillich also calls attention to general revelation, the preparation in culture that made it possible for the church to receive the revelation: "In both the Old and the New Testament we find in language, rites, and in ideas a large element of general revelation as it has occurred and continuously occurs within human religion generally."[6] It is because of this that the history of religion is also considered a theological source. We could not understand the Bible apart from the preparation for it in religion and culture. However, culture and tradition do not have the same weight as sources as scripture. Tradition as a source for Christian theology is not normative because tradition has within it elements that must be judged, and tradition cannot judge itself. The role of tradition is a guiding one: "But tradition can and must be guiding for the theologian, because it is the expression of the continuous reception of the new reality in history and because without tradition, no theological existence is possible."[7] It is erroneous for the theologian to believe that one can jump two thousand years over the Christian tradition and have direct and immediate relationship with the biblical text. The tradition has a guiding role; it mediates between the questions implied in the gospel and the answers that ought to be avoided: "The universality of the Christian claim implies that there is no religion, not even the most primitive, which has not contributed, or will contribute to the preparation and reception of the new reality in history. In this sense the theologian must always be a 'pagan' and a 'Jew' and a 'Greek' [humanist] and bring their spiritual substance under the criterion of the theological norm."[8]

We must now ask, what is the role of experience in doing theology? Tillich speaks of experience as the medium of theology. Without experience, participation in the work of theology would not be possible. Experience is the air theology breathes. However, Tillich is quick to caution that experience is not a source for doing theology. Neither can experience function as the norm for the theological task. The theologian must guard against allowing one's experience that is in part shaped by denominational history and ties to provide the content of theology. The task of the medium is to mediate.

Commenting on the role of experience in the theology of Schleiermacher, Tillich writes:

> *It was the danger of Schleiermacher's theology that his concept of "religious consciousness" became confused with "experience." But it contradicts the basic principle of the Reformation to look at one's self instead of looking beyond one's self at the new reality which liberates man from himself. Our experience is changing and fragmentary; it is not the source of truth, although without it no truth can become* our *truth.*[9]

It is of first importance to note that Tillich stands firmly within the Reformation tradition in his insistence that Christian theology is based on the unique revelation manifested in Jesus as the Christ. The event is not derived from experience but given to experience. In the process of receiving the revelation, experience often colors and even transforms what is given to it but does not provide the source from which it comes. Each religious experience has two sides, the experiential and the revelatory. The revelatory side of a religious experience points to the manifestation of God in human awareness, and it is the grasping of this truth that is critical and crucial for the theologian: "Revelation is the manifestation of the ultimate ground and meaning of human existence (and implicitly in all existence). It is not a matter of objective knowledge, of empirical research or rational inference. It is a matter of ultimate concern; it grasps the total personality and is effective through a set of symbols."[10] It is revelation and not experience that provides the content of theology.

There is, however, an exception to this rule concerning the distinction between experience as form and revelation as content. There is an occasion when both medium and content are identical: it is the point in which subject and object are one. Although it is wrong to call this point God, we must call it "that in us which makes it impossible for us to escape God." We may refer to this as prevenient grace, or the "religious apriori." Tillich goes on, "It is the presence of the element of 'ultimacy' in the structure of our existence, the basis of religious experience."[11]

One of the advantages of regarding experience as a medium rather than source is that not only does it protect the Protestant principle of looking beyond one's self, but in a real way it precludes the possibility of arriving at a new revelation that could somehow transcend the revelation manifested in Jesus as the Christ, which is given to experience. To regard experience as a medium rather than a source protects the final revelation manifested in Jesus as the Christ. The main point that Tillich makes here is that the religious experience should not be allowed to create a new revelation that is discontinuous with the final revelation.

We may ask, however, what if the religious experience enables one to see an aspect of Christian revelation that was not recognized in the past? Would this provide an exception to the rule?

GETTING TO KNOW TILLICH

Ontology is the gateway to Tillich's thought. For him theology does not begin with epistemology but with ontology. His philosophical ontology is composed of four levels: (a) the basic ontological structure, (b) the elements that constitute that structure, (c) the characteristics of being found in existence, and (d) the categories of being and knowing.

For Tillich, the basic ontological structure is the subject/object structure of existence. If a question is asked, there is an asking subject and an object about which it asks. Human beings experience the subject/object structure in terms of the self/world relationship. The self/world structure is the most basic and fundamental of all ontological concepts. The self is not only the unconscious aspects of the ego-self but a centered structure that includes both the central point from which actions and reactions occur and the environment in which the self responds. All reality has centeredness and selfhood. The self is not established by thought but is the basis of thought. Although all reality has selfhood, it is only humanity that has both the capacity and ability to transcend its world through self-consciousness. The ability to use language and engage the universal helps to make this possible. It is not only self/environment that are correlative but self/world: "The self without a world is empty. The world without a self is dead."[12]

The self is not isolated. Human beings experience themselves as having a world to which they belong. The self does not exist in a vacuum. To know oneself is to know that one has a world to which one is united and from which one can retreat. The world has no unity apart from human beings and human beings can have no identity apart from their world. These two realities must be maintained. Each needs the other. Tillich calls attention to the interrelatedness of the ego/world:

When man looks at his world, he looks at himself as an infinitely small part of his world. . . . Without its world the self would be an empty form. Self-consciousness would have no content, for every content, psychic as well as bodily, lies within the universe. There is no self-consciousness without world consciousness, but the converse is also true. World consciousness is possible only on the basis of a fully developed self-consciousness. Man must be completely separated from his world in order to look at his world,

otherwise he would remain in bondage to his world. The
interdependence of ego-self and world is the basic
ontological structure and it implies all others.[13]

Humanity cannot know itself apart from its world. The self/world structure presupposes all other structures. One such structure is "subjective" and "objective" reason. Tillich distinguishes ontological reason from technical reason. *Ontological reason* encompasses the total structure of the mind and universe. He refers to the rational structure of the mind as logos. On the other hand, *technical reason* is reasoning. It provides scientific know-how. The primary concern of the theologian is with ontological reason.

The self/world/subject/object structure of being are composed of three "polar elements": individualization and participation, dynamics and form, freedom and destiny. Individualization, dynamics, and freedom point to the self-relatedness of being; participation, form, and destiny point to the belongingness of being. Whereas the first three polarities point to the self-related aspects of the self-world, the second three point to the world aspect. All of reality participates in these polarities.

Individualization and participation point to the self-centeredness and the belongingness of things. Because individualization and participation are experienced in polar tension, the degree of individualization one realizes depends on the quality of participation. Individualization is not a special characteristic of some beings but a quality of all reality. Individualization implies participation. To be human is to participate. Tillich writes:

The individual self participates in his environment, or
in the case of complete individualization, in his world. An
individual leaf participates in the natural structures and
forces which act upon it and which are acted upon by it. . . .
Man participates in all levels of life, but he participates fully
only in that level of life which he is himself—he has
communion only with persons.[14]

Humanity participates in the universe through its ability to grasp universal structures, forms, and laws. However, humanity's participation is most complete in relation to other human beings. At its deepest level this encounter with other selves is called *communion*. This is participation at its deepest level, since the other is not only capable of offering resistance but can in fact respond with an absolute no.

The second pair of ontological elements are dynamics and form: "Being something means to have a form." It is not possible to think of something without some structure. Tillich asks, "What is this 'something?'" and answers, "We have called it 'dynamics,' a very complex concept with a rich history and many connotations and implications. The problematic character of this concept, and of all concepts related to it, is due to the fact that everything which can be conceptualized must have being, and that there is no being without form. Dynamics, therefore, cannot be thought as something that is; nor can it be thought as something that is not. It is the *me on,* the potentiality of being, which is non-being in contrast to things that have a form, and the power of being in contrast to pure non-being."[15]

So then we could say that dynamics is not something that is, but rather something that is about-to-be. Dynamics is never present by itself but always in relation to form. Dynamics and form point to the capacity and ability of being both to transcend and to conserve itself. Tillich is insistent in his contention that dynamics in humans differ from dynamics in subhuman life, where dynamics is presented as natural necessity. It is only in human life that dynamics reaches out beyond nature. This is what Tillich refers to as vitality: "Vitality is the power which keeps a living being alive and growing. . . . Vitality, in the full sense of the word, is human because man has intentionality. . . . Man is able to create a world beyond the given world; he creates the technical and spiritual realms."[16]

So dynamics and form are experienced in human beings as vitality and intentionality. The term *intentionality* on Tillich's lips points not only to direction but to purpose and meaning. In order to attain and maintain humanity, not only do human beings need the power and drive that keeps human life growing and alive, but human life needs to be related to clusters of meaning.

The third pair of ontological elements are freedom and destiny. This pair of polar elements is of first importance to Tillich, because it is within the framework of these elements that he interprets the Fall, creation, and providence. Freedom and destiny exist in human beings in interdependence. There is no freedom without destiny and no destiny without freedom. Freedom is often spoken of in contrast to necessity. This is misleading, argues Tillich, because the contrast of necessity is possibility. Further, when freedom and necessity are paired together, necessity is thought of as mechanistic determinacy and freedom as indeterministic contingency. This either/or of chance and necessity does not correspond to what human beings experience as freedom: "Man is man because he has freedom, but he has freedom only in polar interdependence with destiny. . . . Man experiences . . . freedom within the larger structures to which the individual structures belong. Destiny points to this situation in which man finds himself, facing the world to which, at the same time, he belongs."[17]

Another reason that Tillich objects to the traditional discussion opposing determinism and indeterminism is that both sides assume that there is a "thing" called "will," which may or may not be free. He contends that a "thing" as pure object is completely determined and therefore by definition lacks freedom. Freedom of a thing is a contradiction of terms. Tillich is insistent that it is not something called "the will" but human beings who are free. Freedom is experienced as deliberation, in which a person is able to weigh arguments and motives, being free of all of them. Further, freedom is experienced as decision, in which real possibilities are "cut off." Each decision is an incision. Finally, freedom is experienced as responsibility, which means that the decisions of human beings are not determined by forces outside of self but reflect a centered self. In each case freedom is bound to the situation in which it is experienced.

When freedom is seen in this context, the meaning of destiny becomes understandable. Destiny is the environment of the self; it is the situation or the context out of which decisions arise. Tillich writes:

> *Our destiny is that out of which our decisions arise; it is the indefinitely broad basis of our centered selfhood; it is the concreteness of our being which makes all our decisions our decisions. . . . It includes the communities to which I belong, the past unremembered and remembered, the environment which has shaped me, the world which made an impact on me. It refers to all my former decisions. Destiny is not a strange power which determines what shall happen to me. It is myself as given, formed by nature, history and myself. My destiny is the basis of my freedom; my freedom participates in shaping my destiny.*[18]

Destiny is not the opposite of freedom; it sets the limits and the conditions of freedom. To be free is to have a destiny. Things do not have destiny because they do not have freedom.

GOD, THE POWER OF BEING

Tillich speaks of God as Being-Itself, the Ground of Being or the Power of Being. The term *Being-Itself* is important for Tillich's theology in that he insists that God is not one being among other beings. God is not even the highest being, or the first cause, because superlatives, when applied to God, become diminutives. Being-Itself is beyond essence and existence. God, who is immanent and at the same time infinite, transcends everything that is, and everything that is participates in God. The immanent God is at the same time the transcendent God.

The concept of God as the power of being is also of first importance for Tillich. God remains God because of God's capacity to take nonbeing into God's self. The power of being that provides the courage to be overcomes sin, guilt, meaninglessness, transitoriness, and death—this power is the power of God. This courage is the presence of God. In *The Shaking of the Foundations* Tillich contends that the traditional ways of talking about God have become empty and irrelevant:

> *The name of this infinite and inexhaustible depth and ground of all being is God. That depth is what the word God means. And if that word has not much meaning for you, translate it, and speak of the depths of your life, of the source of your being, of your ultimate concern, or what you take seriously without reservation. Perhaps, in order to do so, you must forget everything traditional that you have learned about God, perhaps even the word itself. For you know that God means depth, you know much about him. You cannot then call yourself an atheist or unbeliever. For you cannot think or say: Life has no depth! Life itself is shallow. Being itself is surface only. If you could say this in complete seriousness, you would be an atheist; but otherwise you are not. He who knows about depth knows about God.*[19]

God is the beyond in the midst of us. When we pray, we pray to God, who is not only outside of us but within us. We find God close at hand, within us, not above the world but within. Therefore, statements about God are the same as statements about reality.

This attempt to relate God to humanity and to the concrete situation highlights Tillich's attempt to understand the divine life in terms of the ontological elements. In applying the term *individualization* to God, he cautions that God is not the supreme person, but that God is the ground of the personal and participates in every life as its ground and aim. In this sense one could speak of God as the absolute participant. The deistic understanding of God has no place in Tillich's theological framework. So although God is beyond essence and existence, God participates in all of life. God is the divine participant.

Dynamics and form are also applied to the divine life. In the divine life, self-transcendence (dynamics) and self-preservation are completely united. Tillich cautions that we should not think of God in nonsymbolic terms and fall in the error of believing that God has things to do in order to become God. If we did this we would reduce God to "becoming God."

According to Tillich, God holds freedom and destiny in the divine life in perfect harmony. The Bible speaks of the freedom of God, who freely saves, freely creates, and freely reveals: "If we consider the polarity of freedom and destiny in its symbolic value, we find that there hardly is a word said about God in the Bible which does not point directly or indirectly to his freedom. In freedom he creates, in freedom he deals with the world and men and in freedom he saves and fulfills. His freedom is freedom from anything prior to him or alongside him."[20]

But what of destiny? Can destiny be applied to God? Would this not place God in the category with the gods of polytheism that are directed and governed by fate? Or as Tillich poses the question, "Can one say that he who is unconditional and absolute has a destiny in the same manner in which he has freedom? Is it possible to attribute destiny to being itself?"[21] Tillich responds in the affirmative, stating that as long as God is regarded as God's destiny, in God freedom and destiny are one. It is in this sense that God may be spoken of as being God's own law: "If we say that God is his own destiny, we point to the infinite mystery of being and to the participation of God in becoming and in history."[22]

Tillich fleshes out his perception of the divine creativity in terms of a correlation between the divine life and creaturely existence. He rejects the doctrine of creation as an event that took place once upon a time. Rather, creation points to the relationship between God and God's world. Although the doctrine of creation does not describe creation as event, Tillich indicates that there are moments in the creative activity of God that must be maintained: (a) that God has created the world; (b) that God is creative in the present moment; and (c) that God will creatively fulfill his *telos*. This means that we could speak of three moments in creation: (a) originating creation; (b) sustaining creation; and (c) directing creation. God's creativity should not be perceived as an attribute apart from God.

God is not the creator because God creates. God creates because God is the creator. Creation is God's freedom and God's destiny.

GOD'S ORIGINATING CREATIVITY

The first task of theology is to deal with *creatio ex nihilo*. The purpose of understanding creation as *creatio ex nihilo* is that it safeguards the Christian faith from an ultimate dualism. Although the emphasis on *creatio ex nihilo* tends to literalize scripture and focus on the Fall as historical facts of the past, this risk nonetheless ought to be taken. Finitude is not to be equated with the tragic, hence the tragic does not have to be avoided by asceticism. The emphasis on *creatio ex nihilo* also keeps before us the reality and the potentiality but not the necessity of the tragic. Speaking of the doctrine of creation and its relationship to the tragic, Tillich says:

> *The doctrine of creation out of nothing expresses two*
> *fundamental truths. The first is that the tragic character is*
> *not rooted in the creative ground of being; consequently it*
> *does not belong to the essential nature of things. In itself*
> *finitude is not tragic, that is, it is not doomed to self*
> *destruction by its very greatness. Therefore the tragic is not*
> *conquered by avoiding the finite as much as possible, that is*
> *by ontological asceticism. The tragic is conquered by the*
> *presence of being itself with the finite.*[23]

God finds nothing given to God. God creates out of nothing. *Creatio ex nihilo* points in two directions. It can mean the absolute negation of being *ouk on,* or it can mean the relative negation of being *me on.* Tillich rejects both views. He claims that the relative negation would be a recasting of the Greek's view, and the absolute negation of being would not have wrestled with the fact that humanity participates both in being (courage) and nonbeing (anxiety). Tillich writes:

> *The awareness of threatening non-being is anxiety. It is*
> *especially important to distinguish in the case of anxiety the*

objective-psychological and the existentialist use of the term. Anxiety is different from fear, can be observed in animals as well as man. It is a state of anticipation of a negativity without a definite character, and therefore without the possibility of dealing with it in a direct encounter. It is this lack of a definite object which characterizes anxiety in contrast to fear, and it may be (as some neurologists like K. Goldstein say) that only man can have fear, because he alone is able to objectify in a definite way, while both men and animals experience anxiety.[24]

When a person asks, "What is the basis of my being? Why am I not?" that person has envisaged nothingness and applied it to self. If an anticipated event does not appear, one makes a negative judgment that the awaited conditions are nonexistent. This negative judgment implies the distinction between that which is and that which is not, between being and nonbeing. Nonbeing is that which makes it possible for humanity to step back and look at its own being and make that distinction.

Nonbeing is part of being, but what kind of being is it? For Tillich, dynamics is expressed by *me on* or the potentiality of being. Nonbeing is *me on*. It is that which does not yet have being but can become being. On the other hand, *Ouk on* has no relation to being. *Ouk on* is a name for the *nihil,* out of which God created the universe; it is the absolute negation of being. But the nonbeing of which Tillich speaks, *me on,* is different. When Augustine referred to sin as nonbeing, he did not mean that sin has no reality but rather it has only a negative ontological reality; it perverts and resists being. Tillich finds the concept of nonbeing necessary for the articulation of the doctrine of God: "If God is called the living God, if he is the ground of the creative processes of life, if history has significance for him, if there is no negative principle in addition to him which could account for evil and sin, how can one avoid positing a dialectical negativity in God himself?"[25]

The good news is that nonbeing is not another power alongside that of Being-Itself, for in God, nonbeing is continually overcome. In fact, the power of being to overcome nonbeing gives special significance to the divine yes. In human beings, however, nonbeing exists in polar tension with their being and is always present as a danger and a threat. It is possible to succumb to nonbeing and die, or through nonbeing fail to realize one's personality and fully develop. Finite being then is a mixture of being and nonbeing.

SUSTAINING CREATION

God's sustaining creation is made clear in the structures that endure in the midst of change. The laws of nature provide the structures that sustain creation and provide an illustration of the form side of the dynamic form polarity. According to Tillich, God is immanent in the world as its creative ground and transcendent to the world in freedom: "The faith in God's sustaining creativity is the faith in the continuity of the structure of reality as the basis for being and acting."[26]

Tillich calls attention to the inner relatedness of creation, essence, and existence. In actualizing freedom, human beings leave the ground of their being and participate in existence. It is at this point that the connection is made between creation and fall. Tillich puts it cogently:

Being a creature means to be rooted in the creative ground of the divine life and to actualize one's self through freedom. Creation is fulfilled in creaturely self-realization that simultaneously is freedom and destiny. But it is fulfilled through separation from the creative ground through a break between existence and essence. Creaturely freedom is that point at which creation and the fall coincide.[27]

To actualize freedom is to be inside and outside of the divine life at the same time. Tillich contends that God is creative in every moment of existence, giving the power of being to every thing that has being.

Tillich rejects the view of creation that sets a person's happiness or the fulfillment of a need in God as the purpose of creation. This view is refuted by the problem of theodicy. According to Tillich, God is neither a spectator who watches a game called history nor the architect who knows in advance exactly what will happen. He writes:

> *Providence is a permanent activity of God. He never is a spectator; he always directs everything toward its fulfillment. Yet God's directing creativity always creates through the freedom of man and through the spontaneity and structural wholeness of all creatures Providence works through the polar elements of being. It works through the conditions of individual, social and universal existence, through finitude, nonbeing, and anxiety, through the interdependence of all finite things, through their resistance against the divine activity and through the destructive consequences of this resistance.*[28]

Faith in providence is faith in spite of the darkness of fate and the meaninglessness of existence. God uses all factors in creatively directing all things toward their end. Faith in providence is the Christian's answer to the problem of theodicy. God participates in the negativities of existence. This is what incarnation is all about. God is powerful and omnipotent because God resists and overcomes nonbeing. God supplies the ultimate courage that overcomes anxiety.

Eternity does not mean endlessness or everlasting. Rather it points to the presence of God in the past, present, and future: "God's eternity is not dependent on the completed past. For God the past is not complete, because through it he creates the future, and in creating the future he recreates the past. . . . From the point of view of eternity, both past and future are open. The creativity which leads into the future also transforms the past."[29]

Resurrection is the category that best helps Christians understand omnipresence. The doctrine of the omnipresence of God teaches that the world becomes our home and we are not overcome by the anxiety of losing space: "It provides the courage to accept the insecurities and anxieties of spatial existence. In the certainty of the omnipresent God we are always at home and not at home, rooted and uprooted, resting and wandering, being placed and displaced, known by one place and not known by any place."[30]

Tillich concludes his discussion of God with the notion of God as love. He calls attention to four types of love: love as need toward that which completes the need (*libido*), love of the lower for the higher (*philia*), love of equal for equal (*eros*), and finally, love that longs and strives for the fulfillment of the other and affirms the other unconditionally (*agape*). It is the last that is normative of the Christian's understanding of love. Tillich sums up his discourse on love: "Justice is that side of love that affirms the independent right of object and subject within the love relation. Love does not destroy the freedom of the beloved and does not violate the structure of the beloved's individual and social existence. Love as the reunion of those who are separated does not destroy or distort its union."[31] God as love is the final form of the courage to be.

THE NEW BEING

Every age is characterized by a search for a saving power that will heal the disruptions and contradictions of history. Contemporary people experience existence in terms of conflict, self-destruction, meaninglessness, and despair in all areas of life. The question that arises from this situation is not the question of finitude and death as in the ancient Greek church, nor the question of a merciful God and the forgiveness of sins as it was for the reformers. Nor is it the question of personal religious life as in pietism, nor the characterization of society and culture as in the modern age: "It is the question of a reality in which the self-estrangement of our existence is overcome, a reality of reconciliation and reunion, of creativity, meaning and hope. We call such a reality the 'New Being.'"[32]

Tillich begins his discussion of the New Being with essence and existence. *Essence* for him is the standard by which a thing is judged, that which makes a thing what it is. Essence is the power of being and the criterion by which reality is judged. *Existence,* on the other hand, points to what is actual, that which has fallen from essence. Tillich concludes, "The distinction between essence and existence which religiously speaking is the distinction between the created and the actual world, is the backbone of the whole body of theological thought."[33]

The term *New Being* becomes important because it mediates between both essential and existential being. The New Being participates both in the potential character of essential being and in the distorted character of existential being. Christianity claims that the divine life has become incarnate in the life of the man, Jesus the Christ, in the midst of estranged existence. Another way of saying that Jesus the Christ was human and divine, God and man, is to speak of him as New Being—that is, a new reality that is simultaneously essential being and existential being.

Jesus the Christ is essential being in the sense that the power of being is at work in him in a final and decisive way. He participates in existential being in the sense that he was finite, homeless, and lonely. His worldview of the universe was limited to the worldview of his time. He was tempted in all manner just as we are, yet he did not lose his identity with God. Although involved in the ambiguities of life, he was not overwhelmed by them. Another way of talking about existence and essence for Tillich is represented in the symbols of cross and resurrection. Cross represents Jesus subjecting himself to the conditions of existence in the old age, whereas resurrection points to his victory and triumph over the ambiguities of existence (Heb. 4:15).

Tillich raises for us the question regarding the place of research in providing information concerning the Jesus of history. Jesus the Christ is both a historical fact and a faith claim. Jesus the Christ is a historical fact in the sense that he is the event on which Christianity is based. Christ is also a faith claim, because the Christian church came into being with the assertion that Jesus is the Christ. And Jesus the Christ remains the Christ as long as there is a believing community. Tillich comments:

> *Without this reception the Christ would not have been the Christ, namely, the manifestation of the New Being in time and space. If Jesus had not impressed himself as the Christ on his disciples and through them upon all following generations, the man who is called Jesus of Nazareth would perhaps be remembered as a historically and religiously important person. As such he would belong to the preliminary revelation, perhaps to the preparatory segment of the history of revelation. He could then have been a prophetic anticipation of the New Being, but not the final manifestation of the New Being itself. He would not have been the Christ even if he had claimed to be the Christ. The receptive side of the Christian event is as important as the factual side.[34]*

Tillich makes it quite clear that the factual side of the Christ event is not based on historical research aimed at proving the facticity of Jesus as the Christ. According to Tillich this approach and its insistence on empirical verification aimed at proving the truth or falsehood of the Christ event would allow historical research to hold Christianity hostage. Christianity would then have to live with the possibility that one day a new piece of research may disprove the basis on which it is founded. Tillich explains:

> *If the Christian faith is based on a 100,000 to 1 probability that Jesus had said or done or suffered this or that; if Christianity is based on possible birth registers of Nazareth or crime registers of Pontius Pilate, then it has lost its foundation completely. Then the historical event, that a new reality has appeared in mankind and the world (a reality which is reflected in the picture of Jesus as the Christ), has become a matter of empirical verification, ideally through a competent reporter, armed with camera,*

phonograph, and psychography. Since such a reporter, unfortunately, was not available in the year A.D. *30, we have to replace him by more or less probable conjectures. But this is not the historical character of Jesus as the Christ. It is regrettable that one of the greatest events in the history of religion—the radical criticism of the holy legend of Christianity by Christian theologians, which destroyed a whole system of pious superstition—has been abused for the purpose of giving pseudo-scientific foundation to the Christian faith. The historical foundation of theological method does not mean that the theologian has to wait, with fear and trembling, for the next mail which may bring him a new, more critical, or more conservative statement about some important facts of the "life of Jesus" according to which he has to change his faith and his theology. But it does mean that this theology is determined by the event of the appearance of the new reality in history, as reflected in the full biblical picture of Jesus as the Christ and as witnessed by all biblical writers and by the whole tradition of Christianity.*[35]

Tillich is not so much refusing to look with appreciation at the Jesus of history debate but rather prefers to call attention to the centrality of the new reality, the New Being that appeared in Jesus the Christ. What is of first importance here is that in Jesus the Christ, essential being subjected itself to the conditions of existence and overcame it. The paradox of Christianity has to do with the fact that in the personal life of Jesus of Nazareth, the divine Word became incarnate. It is not the personal life of Jesus, as such, that is revelatory, but the New Being mediated through his life: "God can become man, because man is person and because man is personal. And, on the other hand, when God appears in a person, it becomes manifest what person should be."[36] By grounding his theology on what he calls the biblical picture of Christ, Tillich is able to avoid becoming engrossed in the debate concerning the Jesus of history movement.

THE DOCTRINE OF HUMANITY

Tillich speaks of the human situation as existential estrangement. To speak of humanity is to become aware of humanity's relationship and separation from the world. We spoke earlier of the self/world relationship. Humanity is at the same time in the world and outside the world in that the individual self is able to judge the world. Human beings experience finitude and are so able because they participate in infinity. Humanity lives on the boundary between being and nonbeing, between finitude and infinity. People are able to make the transition from essence to existence because they have finite freedom. Through finite freedom they have the capacity and the power to contradict self, to contradict their essential nature. Finite freedom functions within the context of human destiny. The myth of the Garden of Eden is to be understood as dreaming innocence—a dreaming innocence that is driven forward by humanity's awareness of self as limited. This awareness is anxiety. Therefore to be human is to experience "freedom in anxiety."

The desire to sin is fueled by the notion of wanting to preserve dreaming innocence and at the same time actualize freedom. The movement from essence to existence is the original fact. Tillich understands the Fall as a cosmic reality, as a universal fact. The Fall is understood both as transcendent and immanent. The Fall as transcendent reality points to the tragic dimension of sin as destiny, and the Fall as immanent calls attention to the ethical implications of freedom. Another way of speaking of the myths of the Fall as transcendent and immanent is to speak of sin as original and actual. Original sin is destiny, because the shape and form of sin is estrangement. Sin is experienced in the forms of unbelief, pride, and concupiscence. Unbelief points to the rupturing of a relationship with God. It is not so much the fracturing of a relationship with ecclesiastical authority or any other authority as that between God and people. Tillich reminds us that unbelief is a total act. It involves the cognitive, moral, and emotional aspects of the self. Sin as pride is human beings' elevating themselves in the sphere of God. Pride is the correlate of unbelief. It is the turning from God to self as the center of one's life. The reason for wanting to be the center of the world is the desire to draw the rest of the world into self. Tillich calls the craving for unlimited abundance concupiscence. This is a temptation of every individual:

> Man finds himself together with his world in existential estrangement, unbelief, hubris and concupiscence. Each expression of the estranged state contradicts man's essential being, his potency for goodness. It contradicts the created structure of himself and his world and their interdependence. And self-contradiction drives toward self destruction. The elements of essential being which move against each other tend to annihilate each other and the whole to which they belong. Destruction under the conditions of existential estrangement is not caused by some external force. It is not the work of special divine or demonic interferences, but it is the consequence of the structure of estrangement itself.[37]

Evil for Tillich is the structure of destruction. Unbelief, *hubris,* and concupiscence cause certain structures of destruction. The structures of destruction like nonbeing are not caused by external factors but emerge from within estrangement itself and cause chaos. Nonbeing cannot exist without being. Evil cannot exist by itself but is parasitical. Mental illness does not enter the self from outside but from within. Evil then is the consequence of unbelief, *hubris,* and concupiscence on the structure of being. Evil is dependent on the structure of being that it distorts. The main structure of destruction is the disintegration of the center of the self in terms of the self/world polarity. The failure to hold self/world together causes the self to lose its organizing power. In these rare cases, an individual loses his or her world of meanings and values and is determined from without.

In the ideal situation, freedom and destiny exist in a healthy relationship. But under the pull and press of unbelief, *hubris,* and concupiscence, freedom becomes arbitrary and destiny becomes mechanical necessity. And when freedom becomes arbitrary, commitment to a person or cause becomes impossible. Under such circumstances, freedom become compulsiveness while varying and competing motives take over as the self loses centeredness. This Tillich refers to as the bondage of the will:

> To the degree to which freedom is distorted into
> arbitrariness, destiny is distorted into mechanical necessity.
> If man's freedom is not directed by destiny or if it is a series
> of contingent acts of arbitrariness, it falls under the control
> of forces which move against one another without a deciding
> center. What seems to be free proves to be conditioned by
> internal compulsions and external causes. Parts of the self
> overtake the center and determine it without being united
> with the other parts. . . . In view of this "structure of
> destruction," one could say: Man has used his freedom to
> waste his freedom, and his destiny to lose his destiny.[38]

As was mentioned earlier, dynamics and form are expressed in human beings as vitality and intentionality. In estrangement, vitality loses its relation to meaning and becomes an endless striving and questing, always seeking the new and never finding fulfillment. Intentionality, on the other hand, loses its relation to the vital and comes in dry legalisms and fixed social and aesthetic forms. Individualization and participation, under the conditions of existence, point to a person's inability to participate in the world in terms of perception, imagination, and action. A person is cut off, isolated, and lonely.

In the state of estrangement, the categories of time, space, causality, and substance are experienced in terms of resistance and despair. Humanity attempts to prolong its short span of time infinitely in resistance to temporality by filling time with endless activities and by creating for self imaginary worlds of a life after death. When the resistance breaks down, it produces despair. Humanity's failure to accept the finitude of time illustrates its estrangement. In the same way, human beings experience space as contingency, which they attempt to resist by trying to establish for self a fixed place on which to stand physically, psychologically, and culturally in the vain attempt to establish a universal here. Humanity's effort to resist contingency ends in despair.

CONCERNING THE CHURCH AND MINISTRY

For Tillich, the church is the home of Christian theology. Although it is true that theology comes to life in the tension between faith and doubt, the theologian remains a theologian so long as she/he remains committed to the theological circle. The theologian is accountable to the church. The philosopher may follow truth wherever it leads, oblivious of the community to which she/he belongs, but not the theologian. The theologian functions within the context of the church.

However, we must ask, and Tillich informs us that a critical question that concerns the church is, how may the church relate to the situation in which it finds itself without losing its power. One way in which the church could ensure the capacity to relate to its context is to have a theology that expresses ultimate concern and a spiritual center of religious beliefs. The church must guard against becoming the servant of a social and cultural system. Through its symbols, the church is able to preserve its distinctive message despite all secular and ecclesiastical distortions: "Christianity is not only part of the contemporary world; it is also protest against it and an effort to transform it by the power of the Christian faith."[39]

In a trenchant article, "The Relevance of Ministry in Our Time and Its Theological Foundation," Tillich cautions against the dangers of the church and its ministers becoming irrelevant. The good news is that neither can become completely irrelevant, or the question of the renewal and revitalization of the church would be precluded. It is because the Christian message stands for something of ultimate significance that precludes it from being held captive by the situation. Although the message is in culture, it transcends all cultural expressions. The church and its ministry are often considered irrelevant because they have no essential relation to that for which they claim relevance. The question of the church and its ministry, however, applies not only to those inside the church but also to those outside the church.

The principle of the priesthood of all believers has sought to remove the hierarchical position of the ministry. This approach to ministry has removed the priesthood as a sacramentally consecrated elite but has not removed the function of the minister. On the contrary, it has given to the minister the highest function that Protestantism knows, namely to preach the Word, which includes the administration of the sacraments. In Protestantism, every Christian lay person can perform these activities in principle. As soon as the minister acts in this way, she/he acts as a priest and the question of the relevance of the ministry applies to her or him. Every Christian can become a priest for another Christian.

If we hold that the task of the minister is to pronounce, preach, teach, and in counseling mediate the Word of God, then the question of the relevance of the ministry for every human being becomes more intelligible. The *Word of God* means the self-manifestation of that which concerns everyone ultimately. And according to Tillich, nothing could be more relevant than that which concerns one ultimately. So if the ministry of the Word of God has become irrelevant, it means that the Word of God is being taught and proclaimed in such a way that it is not understood and received as a matter of ultimate concern by the people of our time.

The sense of the irrelevance of the church in society then has to do with the inability of the church to speak to the people of a largely secularized world in such a way that they feel the message concerns them ultimately, that the ministry is a matter of "to be or not to be." This is the case in spite of the fact that the church has a very able and trained clergy. Their encounter with the world raises difficult conflicts that they are unable to deal with sometimes. Tillich writes:

> *The word [gospel] does not mean that the functions*
> *falling under this judgement are irrelevant; but it does mean*
> *that they are not able to make the ministry relevant as*
> *ministry. This refers to the social, the political, the*

educational, the psychotherapeutic activities of ministers.
They are all relevant for human life. But none of them
represents the meaning of ministry as ministry. None of them
makes the minister relevant as minister. It is not unimportant
that there are groups (congregation) who, under the
directions given by the minister, provide some kind of
community for people who would otherwise remain lonely. It
is not unimportant that congregations provide occasions
where people can eat together, play together, discuss and
dance together in an atmosphere which stands under the
judgement of Christian principles. But from the point of view
of the meaning of ministry, all this is pseudo-relevant. It has
the tendency to cover up the basis for the minister's claim to
be relevant. It makes him into the director of social activities
in a service club, and it often prevents him from
concentrating on the function which should make him
relevant—that of pronouncing and repeating the message of
the new reality.[40]

The church has great relevance in relation to political organizations. And it is of utmost importance that the church be heard in the arena of public life. Tillich describes one of the church's shortcomings, especially in Europe, as the neglect of the responsibility of mediating the Gospel in public affairs. In a profound sense the church has to do more than mediate the Gospel through pronouncements, preaching, and the administration of the sacraments and counselling. It has to be the bearer of the Word in public life as well.

When the church speaks to public life, however, it must speak as the church: "The relevance of the ministry lies not in its political utterances, nor in their possible value, but in its representation of the sources from which such utterances come." When the church works as a political pressure group, it does what other agencies are able to do, whereas no other group is able to do what the church does. The key to the church's relevance is in embodying and proclaiming the

New Being manifested in Jesus as the Christ and on which the very existence of the church is based.

Even the educational activities of the ministry do not make it relevant as ministry. A minister may become a college president or leader in an educational association, but this does not make him/her relevant as minister of the gospel. As a minister he/she represents the New Being from which educational consequences may be drawn by him/her or by others. The primary task of the minister is to communicate the healing power of the Christian faith, which is the power of the reconciliation of the estranged and the reunion of the separated.

The relevance of the Christian ministry will also be decreased if along with their function as club directors, pressure group agents and educators, many of our ministers consider themselves psychologists. The Christian ministry is relevant to our time insofar as it is able to communicate the message of the new reality as an answer to the questions implied in human existence. This is a task of insuperable difficulty, however, and could not be implemented if it were dependent on the goodwill of the ministers and theologians alone.

But this is not the case—"history shuts and opens doors." It was the development of an independent secular culture in the Western world that pushed the ministry into a corner. In the view of industrial society, the Christian message is a strange body of different forms of life and thought. Tillich contends that this can be seen in the many attempts to analyze our culture from sociological, psychological, and philosophical perspectives. The dimension of depth and height is sacrificed to the horizontal dimension.

In this culture one does not look up and down, but one looks ahead in all directions. But the Christian message came out of the vertical dimension and seeks to turn humankind in the direction of depth and height. Wherever it is truly heard, it makes a qualitative difference. But it is not heard, because humanity determined by the world as it is shaped by industrial society shuts the self off from the vertical dimension, the dimension of the ultimate in meaning and being. Hence, Christianity becomes superficial and an emotional outlet.

Tillich then examines the ways in which the church has reacted to the secular culture that has pushed it into irrelevance. The church has adopted two approaches. On the one hand, it has attempted a radical rejection of the culture, and on the other hand, it has practiced a radical adaptation to culture. According to Tillich, the church has failed on both counts, and both approaches are partly responsible for the irrelevance of ministry today. In applying the method of radical rejection, the church seeks to preserve its life through the practice of orthodoxy in Europe and fundamentalism in America. The attempt at radical adaptation expresses itself in theological humanism and liberal theology on both continents. These approaches tend to make the Gospel inaccessible and superfluous. The challenge facing the church is to find another way that is both meaningful and approachable.

The Christian minister has a responsibility to relate the changeless message of the gospel to the everchanging situation. The minister needs to keep in mind that the Christian ministry is one of reconciliation. It is an occasion for concern that one can find in the words of the psychological helper a ministry of reconciliation and not in the words of the minister. Moralistic preaching does not help people caught in a tension between what they are and what they ought to be. When the minister becomes the articulator of a moralistic gospel, his or her preaching lacks the power of the gospel of reconciliation. Moralistic preaching does not aid people in a situation of despair about themselves. On the contrary, it drives them into deeper despair or into a compromise about their actual being and what they feel ought to be. The minister as a mere representative of the moral law has pseudo-relevance but lacks the relevance and power of one who has the message of reconciliation.

Another problem arises for the minister when the symbols of atonement are communicated in a language that has no meaning to the secular world. Tillich contends that it is possible for contemporary people to understand a description of the human situation in terms of an analysis of guilt and despair: "The relevance of the crucified lies not in a theology of the cross but in a vision of the crucified."[41] The most challenging task confronting the minister is to make the Christological symbolism relevant to the people of our time. If the minister is unable to show the universal human significance of the Christian message in its particularity, he remains irrelevant for our time. The most accurate indicator of the predicament of our time is not so much the attempt to overcome the secular or the conquest of guilt but the attempt to come to grips with meaninglessness. This is a direct consequence of our secular culture and its manifestation of emptiness. The main test for ministry today is the overcoming of emptiness and the providing of meaning for our lives.

TILLICH AND KING

It is somewhat surprising that Martin Luther King Jr. and Paul Tillich never met, especially because the last ten years of Tillich's life were years of great visibility for both King and Tillich on the national and global stage. Tillich had come to great notoriety as he dominated Protestant theology in the United States and shared the global stage with Karl Barth until his death in 1965. Martin Luther King Jr., through his leadership of the civil rights movement, had become a household name throughout the United States.

It is to King's credit that he initiated a correspondence with Tillich. He sought to meet with Tillich in order to discuss his dissertation at Boston University, "A Comparison of the Conceptions of God in the Thinking of Paul Tillich and Henry Nelson Weiman." Tillich, writing from Sweden, was appreciative of King's inquiry and offered to meet with King, but somehow their schedules did not make it possible. King, however, immersed himself in Tillich's thought in completing his dissertation. Writing to his wife from Reidsville State Prison, he asked her to bring him, among other books, Tillich's *Systematic Theology,* volumes 1 and 2.

King's approach to theology is not as academic as Tillich's. King did not practice theology in the classroom but made his theology in the streets, at rallies with sanitation workers, or in jail (as his

"Letter from Birmingham Jail" indicates). Nonetheless, King seems to take Tillich's method and approach seriously. First, King, like Tillich, articulates a method of correlation. Theology for him calls attention to the partnership between divine and human agency. King's speeches are replete with the call: we for God and God for us. According to King, whenever human beings cooperate with God, there is no struggle where victory is not assured: God needs us and we cannot be without God. This divine/human encounter that is the hallmark of Tillich's theology is emblematic of King's attempt to talk about the divine participation in human affairs.

According to King, a Black minority outside the mainstream of American life could take on the American system and demand human rights not only because it was their God-given right but also because the God of the universe participated with them. Something of a covenantal theology anchored in an understanding of reconciliation seems to be the bedrock of King's theology. This is not much different from the theology of Tillich, except that Tillich's view of reconciliation includes all elements of existence. For Tillich, the whole created order groans and travails for the answer in revelation. It is here, at one level, that we begin to get a feel for the difference between their approaches to theology, beyond the claim that Tillich's view is more philosophical, academic, and complete. It is from where the emphasis is placed in the theological task that we receive a glimpse of the distinctiveness of each contribution.

Both theologians eschew a covenantal theology anchored in the quest for reconciliation. Both theologians have as a presupposition of the theological task an inclusive covenant. For both, God is the ground and the power of being for everything that has being. And both begin with the existential pole of the correlation. Both theologians insist on the need for analysis of the situation and the importance of God's Word providing the answer.

One of the primary differences in approaches concerns the fact that King gives sociological concreteness to the situation in a way that Tillich's system and technical language do not allow. As I observe in chapter 5 on King, although Tillich focuses on the world situation, King concentrates on a particular situation; consequently, we cannot find any reference in Tillich's work to the civil rights movement that King led in this country, and Tillich did not give us any revolutionary principle to help us question oppression in a theological way. In a sense, this was Tillich's blind side. This is most unfortunate, because the early writings, which we have not considered since our main focus is to put Tillich's work in America in conversation with King's, were praxis-oriented and gave a great deal of time and energy to the plight and predicament of the oppressed.

Both Tillich and Barth were young socialists and wrote essays extolling the socialist values and indicating why socialism was not antithetical to Christianity. A "Kairos Circle," founded in 1920, provided a context for Tillich's political and theological work.[42] It is unfortunate that while on the American scene he neglected to involve his theology in the plight of the oppressed, since he was no stranger to their concerns. In this one area King's theological focus certainly differs from that of Tillich: an insistence that theology be involved in the particularities of the situation at hand. Because Tillich insisted on speaking from a universal theological perspective, his theology remains focused on generalities.

Perhaps the main difficulty that King had with Tillich was Tillich's doctrine of God. King makes it quite clear in his dissertation that both Tillich and Weiman had no problems articulating and substantiating the reality of God. The problem had to do with what they sacrificed in trying to prove that God transcends existence, that God is not one being among other beings. King contends that what they gave up was the notion of the personal God. It is not enough to speak of God as the ground of the personal; God *is* personal, contends King. King argues that the danger with Tillich's view of God is that it minimizes the religious value. Because of this Tillich could not see God as a person; to see God in this light was to set limits to God.

King believes that personality is an adequate category for talk about God, because personality as such does not have limitations. The essence of personality for King is self-direction and self-awareness. The main problem, argues King, is whether or not one could worship Tillich's God or place trust in this God. The emotion to worship God and trust God presupposes the personality of God. It is difficult to trust in and have communion with Being-Itself or a "creative event." King concludes that Tillich's view of God is too abstract and abstruse. Speaking of God as personal, King writes:

> To say that this God is personal is not to make him a finite object beside other objects or attribute to him the limitation of human personality; it is to take what is finest and noblest in our consciousness and affirm its perfect existence in him. It is certainly true that human personality is limited, but personality us such involves no necessary limitations. It means simply self-consciousness and self-direction. So in the truest sense of the word, God is a living God. In him there is feeling and will, responsible to the deepest yearnings of the human heart: this God both evokes and answers prayer.[43]

In his important book *Roots of Resistance,* William Watley argues that King could not accept Tillich's view of God because in "black religious thought God is a being with personality, who can be loved as well as rejected, praised and worshipped as well as denied. When forces of dehumanization and oppression are confronted daily, when the environment is perceived essentially as hostile rather than supportive, blacks must have a God who personally cares for them, who hears their cries, understands their sorrows, and assures them of divine presence and help in times of distress.[44] While noting that King's acquaintance with Bostonian personalism provided a catalyst for King's thought in his critique of Tillich's theology, Watley nonetheless points out that it was King's grounding in the Black church that ultimately made Tillich's view of God unacceptable to him.

The central question for King was not does God exist? but rather does God care? This was the bottom line for King because it has always been the critical issue for the Black church. In a culture and community in which the assault of slavery tore many families asunder, it was important to affirm that "God is a mother to the motherless, and a father to the fatherless." For these families the church became home, and God was the head of the family. For a people who were cut off from their historical and cultural roots, God was their father and mother. This caring personality could be relied upon to protect and provide. David Garrow, in *The FBI and Martin Luther King, Jr.,* supports Watley's view of Black religious thought as he calls attention to King's growing confidence in the God who cares, an understanding of God that was nurtured in the Black church. Garrow writes:

> *In the last year and one-half of King's life a good number of his sermons ended with a refrain that articulated his deepest sentiments. God, he stated, would not desert one even if everything was going badly, even if criticism was coming from all sides, and even if hope for a better future had grown very dim. One must hold on to some amount of faith, for "he promised never to leave me, never to leave me alone, never alone, no never alone. He promised never to leave me, never to leave me alone."* [45]

Although Tillich's God was ultimately too impersonal to satisfy King's theology, Karl Barth's God was too transcendent, too "wholly other." Examining Barth's theology and its relationship to King's thought is the task of the following chapter.

CHAPTER 3 KARL BARTH'S PERSPECTIVE

It is quite common to hear theologians refer to Barth as a theologian of revolution. Barth's revolution was not through the upheaval of social structures but through the quest for liberation in church and tradition. Contrary to traditional methods of theology, Barth does not begin with general and epistemological considerations about the nature and existence of a supreme being. He begins at the beginning with the reality of God that precedes and constitutes the basis for the reality of people, including their desire to know and to serve God.

It was in the struggle to minister to his congregation and to preach to them faithfully that the theological revolution of our time was born. After being assistant minister in the German-speaking church at Geneva, at the age of twenty-five, Karl Barth went to Safenwil in 1911, where he took his duties and responsibilities as pastor with the utmost seriousness. Safenwil contained a sawmill, a dye factory, and a weaving plant. Barth became involved in the life of a community in which people were struggling to move from rural patterns of life to an industrialized economy. Not only was Barth a member of the Social Democratic Party fighting the cause of women workers in the local knitting factory, he was also telling the workers in sermons and addresses that the God of the Western world was finished.

He also supported the factory workers in their struggle for

better working conditions. The level of Barth's involvement on behalf of the workers was so intense that his parishioners nicknamed him the "red pastor." He tried to organize unions for the poorly paid textile workers and refused to acknowledge the distinction between rich and poor. As a member of the Social Democratic Party along with Paul Tillich and others, he believed that the socialist movement was a cause of great religious importance, destined to become an instrument for realizing God's dominion on earth.

During the first five years at Safenwil, Barth made no serious break with the liberal theology learned from von Harnack and Herrmann. He broke no new ground. He gave his time to two activities· preaching and helping a major social problem in his parish. Although many of Barth's parishioners were farmers, there were also many parishioners who worked at the three factories in Safenwil. As a pastor he also had to deal with the problems of management and labor. Barth, however, was not left to handle these problems by himself. In 1913 his good friend Eduard Thurneysen became pastor in the nearby village of Leutwil. Together they were quickly drawn to the side of the laborers and plunged themselves into all the problems of legislation, unions, and management.

During this time Barth encountered "the strange new world of the Bible." He began to see himself as one who was called to listen to the Word of God and in a new way to give heed to God's word. His desire to preach conflicted with his sense of the awesome responsibility attached to preaching: could he in fact dare to preach? It was here that his friend and neighbor Eduard Thurneysen helped him to become aware of the attitude of the people of the Bible. According to Thurneysen, one encountered in the Bible, especially among the prophets and apostles, people who did not allow the ecclesiastical environment and life to define them. These people were able to transcend their setting. With these people there was no passion for religious experience merely for the sake of getting an experience, nor any attempt to stand on an even keel with God. Rather there was a deep reverence and consciousness that reminded them of "the infinite qualitative distance between them and God."

Barth noted the many ways in which the people of the Bible stopped in their tracks and gave time and attention to God. Barth found himself wanting to listen more to the Word of God. In this "strange new world of the Bible," no one doubted the irremovable contrast between life and death, life and eternity, the creator and the created. Everyone looked up, and his or her sole purpose was to give glory to God. In the Bible, Barth met people who encountered God and somehow had been taken hold of by God, and these people abandoned the great godlessness of the attempt to make themselves like God. Barth learned for himself the trembling of Jeremiah. It was in the light of the Bible he saw the position out of which he must speak, the position of one who, like Abraham, finds himself thrown upon the grace of God, in which he alone can find a place to stand. Barth tells us that it was in St. Paul that he first found help, so in the next few years he gave himself to a study of the Pauline Epistles, especially to the Epistle to the Romans.

KARL BARTH AND SOCIALISM

In a letter to Thurneysen on 11 November 1918, Barth writes:

If only we had been converted to the Bible earlier so that we would now have solid ground under our feet: One broods alternately over the newspaper and the New Testament and actually sees fearfully little of the organic connection between the two worlds concerning which one should now be able to give a clear and powerful witness. Or is it different for you?[1]

For Barth the New Testament and the newspaper represent two worlds that cannot be separated. This is because any theory about the subject of the New Testament is at heart a theory of praxis made plain in the present. In his second edition of *The Epistle to the Romans,* Barth comments on Romans 12:1: "I appeal to you, therefore, brethren." According to Barth, "Paul is not here turning his attention to practical religion, as though it were a second thing side by side with the theory of religion. On the contrary, the theory, with which we have hitherto been concerned, is the theory of the practice of religion."[2]

The suffering of the people in his congregation, the plight of the women workers, and the tensions between management and labor all forced Barth to deal with the concrete problems in his parish. From the beginning of his ministry in Safenwil, he addressed the Workers' Union on "Human Rights and Civil Duties" and during this period published his lecture, "Jesus Christ Is the Social Movement." Barth saw a correlation between Jesus Christ and the social movement. For him Jesus Christ is the social movement and the social movement is Jesus Christ. In this article Barth responds to different levels of criticism in his attempt to link Jesus Christ and the social movement. He counters the arguments of those from what he terms narrow Christian circles, who challenge that Jesus Christ could possibly have anything in common with the social movement. Criticism also came from the labor movement, which feared that the link with Christianity would tend to make the movement too conservative, effectively asking the union members to become church members also.

The narrow Christian critique contends that Jesus does not belong to any party and is therefore apolitical. Jesus Christ is above culture. To relate Jesus Christ to a political movement is to "profane the eternal." Invariably critics would cite a listing of the failings of the movement and ask what honest Christian in good conscience could say that Jesus Christ has anything to do with all this. Barth retorts that it is not fair to judge a movement by what it does. Rather a movement should be judged by what its goals are. Christians in particular should know this because they are insistent that Christianity should not be judged by what Christians do but by the goals of Christianity. He contends that to ask what Social Democrats want is already to ask about the Eternal Word that became flesh in Jesus Christ. It is in this sense that one can begin to see an inner connection between social democracy and the Gospel.

To the critique that presumes that Christians want to convert

Social Democrats, Barth admits that it might appear that way but that is in fact quite far away from the case since he has no such intention. He is convinced that to know Jesus Christ does not mean to be converted to a set of beliefs or doctrine. When one sees the connection between one's socialist convictions and Jesus Christ, one begins to realize that what Jesus brings us is not ideas, not even new ideas, but a way of life. There are many people who have Christian ideas about God and the world and humanity, and yet they are still "heathens." To follow Jesus is not at all the same as subscribing to a worldview. Therefore one can be an atheist and a follower of Jesus at the same time. One should not equate Jesus with ideas about him or with doctrines and dogmas about him. All ideas about him and dogmas and doctrines must be subordinated to him and the praxis that issues forth out of an encounter with him.

Karl Barth begins to sound like a liberation theologian as he speaks more directly of the relationship between Jesus Christ and socialism. He sees both as a movement from below. Socialism, the movement of the proletariat, works from below and moves upward insofar as it seeks independence for the dependent. Jesus Christ, when seen from the human perspective, is thoroughly a movement from below. Jesus Christ, Barth points out, came from the lower social stratum of society. The movement of Jesus was "a volcanic eruption from below." For Barth, Jesus' teaching on the dominion of God calls into question the tendency to see the dominion of God as spiritual, internal, and otherworldly. Because of this the church often assigns politics to the world and preaches conversion where social democracy teaches revolution.

According to Barth, Jesus knows nothing of this bifurcation in reality. His teaching does not represent two worlds but one reality that is represented in the dominion of God. This reality finds opposition not in the world, not in matter, not in the external but in evil, in the devil who lives within. The dominion of God comes to us in the real world. The Word became flesh (John 1:14). The socialist seems to take more seriously the prayer that Christians pray, "Our Father," than do Christians. They work more energetically than Christians to make this prayer a reality in our world.

But Jesus is more a socialist than the socialists. Whereas the socialists advocate the abolition of private ownership of the means of production, Jesus demands the abolition of all private ownership. According to Barth, Jesus insists that we become free of everything that begins with "I" and "my." Barth saw solidarity as the law and gospel of socialism, indicating that Jesus' "Our Father" points up that for Jesus there existed only a social God of solidarity and therefore a religion of solidarity. Here Barth criticizes the church's penchant for the religion of individualism and its emphasis on the private relationship between God and the soul. In the cross as Jesus laid down his life for others, we find the highest value that one can conceive in life. In this expression we find the consciousness of solidarity, the basis of being human. One must be willing to lose self in order to find self.

In a letter dated 5 February 1915, Barth writes to his friend Eduard Thurneysen about his formally becoming a member of the Social Democratic Party:

> *I have now become a member of the Social Democratic Party. Just because I set such emphasis Sunday by Sunday upon the last things, it was no longer possible for me personally to remain suspended in the clouds above the present evil world but rather it had to be demonstrated here and now that faith in the Greatest does not exclude but rather includes within it work and suffering in the realm of the imperfect. The socialists in my congregation will now, I hope, have a right understanding of my public criticisms of the party. And I myself hope now to avoid becoming unfaithful to our "essential" orientation as might very well have happened to me had I taken this step two years ago.*[3]

Barth's membership in the party did not blind him to the party's faults and weaknesses. He saw socialism just as much compromised as liberal theology but somehow expected more from socialism than from the church in relation to the war. He felt that it was more likely that socialism would take a stand against the war than the Christian church. It was to his great disappointment that he saw it doing the very opposite, so quite early after he joined the party he began to put together an article on "The Intrinsic Future of Social Democracy." Although there were problems with the party, Barth proceeded to look for and to make a case for the party's future.

There are three things that the party must keep in mind if it is to return to its revolutionary character. Socialism must identify its essence, its means, and its goal. The debate as to whether or not socialism had a spirit was resolved for Barth as he answered yes to that question. But he wanted to see socialism develop a new social disposition. This press and pull for a new social disposition was to be the overarching rubric if socialism was to recapture its revolutionary praxis. For this to happen, socialism must regard justice for humanity as its essence and content. The task of socialism was not to merely improve the condition of the working class. The passion for justice for every worker and every person must be the mainspring of socialism rather than its attempt to value persons on the basis of works. Barth contended that this was one area in which socialism was compromising itself.

Barth was concerned with the issue of the source from which socialism drew its strength. The strength should not come from the struggle for political or economic power. Its strength should be drawn from its trust in the power of truth. Failure to do this will aid in the compromising of the party.

The aim of socialism should be the free, pure personality, and the future state should be a means to the attaining of that end. Personality is to be set free from bourgeois egoism, with its false idealism and half-serious Christianity. These principles for the establishment of a new social disposition within socialism would provide a creative basis for the renewal of the party. The same year, in 1915, Karl Barth wrote an article, "Religion and Socialism," in which he pointed out that he became a socialist because he was glad to be a pastor, not because he was bored with being a pastor. He understood his calling to be a pastor as the main thing and regarded it as the basis for social and political action. His political choices sprang from his theological existence and theological commitments.

His understanding of the dominion of God was the basic theological premise. Socialism was a reflection of the dominion, as was the Reformation, the Enlightenment, the Renaissance, or the French Revolution. The pastoral calling is concerned with the fact of the dominion of God and working for the dominion. Even religion Barth sees as a reflection of the dominion of God. He sees religion as an anthropological point of departure as it constitutes a response to the dominion of God. The title "Religion and Socialism" is indeed inappropriate since religion and socialism reflect the same order. It becomes more appropriate then to speak of "The Kingdom of God and Socialism," since the dominion of God provides a basis for critiquing socialism.

Here we get a hint at a new theological starting point that was to emerge for Barth. He has made a shift from 1911 in which he argued that Jesus is the socialist movement. In 1915 he would not think of equating the dominion of God with socialism. He is a socialist not as a pastor but as a human being and a citizen. Socialism is a signpost of the dominion of God, a clue that God is at work in God's world. By calling attention to the distinctive difference between religion and the dominion of God, Barth is able to show that the dominion of God, which is the rule of God, is where God is at work. Barth was convinced that God was at work in the world in many ways quite apart from religion, and that one ran the risk of being apart from God if one did not join God in these movements. One such occasion to join God was socialism.

For Barth, theology is concerned with real life situations and is therefore a theory of praxis. Religion for him has an anthropological focus, whereas the dominion of God, worldly in that it points to the basic fact of life, also highlights the rule of God in this world. Socialism points to the human praxis that calls attention to God's work in the world. Because as a pastor Barth sees his primary commitment to the dominion of God, he refuses to identify himself as a "political pastor" or a "religious pastor" in the sense that he is called to serve the political interests or the religious interests of any society.

BARTH AND ROMANS

Barth seems to have felt the need for more, and so in 1916 he began work on his commentary on Romans. The first edition was published in 1919 with a clear theme of dynamic eschatology, the movement from a doomed temporal order to a restored order ruled by God. The book is an affirmation of the sovereignty of God and God's faithfulness and salvation in Jesus Christ.

Hans Urs von Balthasar indicates in his important book *The Theology of Karl Barth* that the conceptual framework is derived from Plato, Hegelianism, and religious socialism. According to Plato, the world displays a threefold movement: existence in the idea, break off from the idea, and return to the idea. Christianity took over this framework and modified it in two ways. Existence in the idea becomes spirit, break off from the idea becomes psyche, the realm of the soul.

Remembrance of the original homeland does not provide the power to restore the soul to the rightful place. These Christian modifications of Platonism do not address the central issue: the notion of existence in the idea. For Christians, existence is not in an idea but in God. When God sets out to restore humankind, God's own Spirit steps in and does the restoration. The redeemed becomes the foundation for the life of each and every individual. So humanity, which broke away from God, recalls its origins and at the same time recalls its own transcendental being and God. Humanity is summoned to become what humanity really is.

The breakaway is the result of humanity's desire to establish independence vis-à-vis God. Humanity breaks away from direct existence with God. Humanity wants to be like God, to be self-important in its own right. The desire to exist of oneself means separation from God and this move is sin. Distance between the creature and God represents the creature's separation from God.

Hence the principle of analogy, which expresses this distance, is equated with the breaking away. The person who is separated from God's Spirit becomes flesh. This new condition is an offense in itself. It is the root of multiplicity. It sets up opposition between life and the ideal and is the source of death, illusion, untruth, nonbeing, and chaos.

Barth insisted that the time had come to read the Bible differently. The challenge was not to ask what Paul meant for his contemporaries but rather what Paul means for us today. So Barth became impatient with the historical critical method. His insistence was that in the same way Paul spoke directly to the first century so his message comes directly to the twentieth. Barth is not unaware of the importance of faithful exegesis, but of far more significance is the truth that as prophet and apostle of the dominion of God he speaks to every person of every age.

Barth did not allow his publishers to reprint the first edition. We are told that after a meeting with Gogarten in Barth's home, Barth decided to rewrite the book. And so a new edition appeared in the early months of 1922. In the preface he informs us that he completely rewrote the book after a careful study of such diverse scholars as Paul, Overbeck, Plato, Kant, Kierkegaard, and Dostoyevsky. He seeks very early to answer his critics. Jülicher criticized the first edition for being theological. Barth affirms that he is a theologian and never sought to be any thing but a theologian. In fact, one area in which both commentaries are alike is that they are unashamedly theological works. He responds to those who charged that the first edition was not simple enough. Here Barth points out that he had no intentions of trying to be simple, because the understanding of God in the Bible was not a simple matter. The challenge as he saw it was not so much to speak simply as it was to speak the truth.

Barth claims that it is to misunderstand him to see him as an enemy of biblical criticism. The problem that he has with biblical criticism is that it does not go far enough. It often stops short of the actual understanding and interpretation of the document. To compare Jülicher with Calvin, Barth claims, bears out his point. Because Jülicher treats Paul as ancient history, he really does not come to grips with any meaningful interpretation of Paul's thought. This is not the case with John Calvin, who is able to rethink Paul's thoughts until the walls that separate the first and the sixteenth centuries come tumbling down. The challenge is for the critic to become more critical in order that the message of the document may become alive and available for the church. Justice is not being done in theological education, claims Barth, because students are not being trained to impart the Scripture in a way that preaching demands. Rather they stand in awe of history and are often incapable of pointing to the Word of God hidden in human words.

Hans Urs von Balthasar helps us understand the continuity between the two editions of Romans. The pathos of the distance between God and creation takes us back to the notion of original *identity* that we encountered in the first edition. Also present in the second edition is the focus on "remembrance" of our "lost intimacy with God," our "direct unity with God." Another theme present in both works is that of the creature breaking away as the creature acquires self-awareness. Human beings were not meant to be a second reality alongside God. We were not to know the secret that God knew and mercifully hid from humanity that we are only human. Here the law of distance, the law of analogy, is sin. To be creatures means to be guilty; however, salvation in Christ means return to unity. In Christ we see what being a person means in God's eyes: hell, death, abandonment of God. Christ steps in Adam's place and Adam is each one of us.

Hans Urs von Balthasar sums up the contribution of the second edition of *Romans:*

> *Only against the backdrop of a presupposed original identity does the whole dialectic of Romans become possible. The pathos of distance, through the pages of the second edition, does not change the fact. Once again identity results in the elimination of the concept of nature. On the one side, nature again coincides with grace, since they are of one and*

the same origin: "where every thing natural is holy by that
very fact, because the Holy, too, is natural." On the other
side, the very personality of man coincides with the Holy
Spirit, the new in Christ.[4]

DIALECTICAL THEOLOGY

While revising his manuscript on *The Epistle to the Romans* in
1921, Barth was invited to fill the position in the newly created chair
of Reformed Theology in the Lutheran faculty at Göttingen. Early in
1922, the University of Münster awarded him an honorary Doctorate
of Theology. The first years were especially challenging for Barth
because he had to acquire a grounding in historical theology, which
he had somewhat neglected as a pastor. His first courses were on the
Heidelberg Catechism and on Ephesians (on which he had done
some work as a pastor).

The Reformation became a critical key for him. He gave particular attention to Calvin and the history of dogma. Most of his reading outside of the era of the Reformation was really to help him
better understand the Reformation. In the meantime, his revised
Romans was published and became a best-seller. This made Barth
very visible and greatly in demand as a lecturer. Some of the lectures
he worked on during this period were published in 1928 in the
collection *The Word of God and the Word of Man.*

While working on Calvin at Göttingen, Barth became a systematic theologian. He spent a great deal of time on such questions as:
What is the relationship between the Reformation and Schleiermacher? In what way was the Reformation responsible for Schleiermacher's book *The Christian Faith*? Why did Schleiermacher and
his theology exist at all? If Schleiermacher and his theology were
taken away would there be left a gap in the history of Protestantism?

Barth felt that there was room for a fresh beginning, that a clue
to this fresh start lay somewhere in the reexamination of the doctrine
of the Trinity, and that Holy Scripture ought to provide the controlling key. But for now he was busy with preparations for class. It was
one thing to want to set Protestant theology on a fresh path and to

isolate the weaknesses in Reformation theology that opened the door for the emergence of Schleiermacher, and quite another to be about the business of constructing a new theology. In the meantime, he immersed himself in the history of dogmatics. In 1927, he published *Christian Dogmatics in Outline* (volume 1), *The Doctrine of the Word of God: Prolegomena to Christian Dogmatics.*

This was a trial run for Barth. The strident voice we hear in *Church Dogmatics* is absent here. However, his passion and experience as pastor are evident as there are sections on preaching, the Bible, and Revelation. Themes such as "God in the sermon," "The Word of God and Man as Preacher," and the threefold form of the Word of God as Proclamation, Canon, and Revelation are explored. These themes were to be picked up again in *Church Dogmatics*. The themes of preaching, listening, and believing provided concrete context and gave sociological concreteness to the doctrine of Revelation. So Barth had not yet left Schleiermacher behind, and perhaps for the rest of his life, his struggle with Schleiermacher would continue.

Insofar as religion is the point of departure for theological reflection or for humanity's understanding of self, it is the enemy of revelation. According to Barth, religion gives to people a false sense of who they are in that it makes them feel comfortable in the presence of God rather than uncomfortable because of sin. Humanity is tempted to idolatry and the hope of losing the self in the divine life through mystical contemplation. The danger here is that the I/thou between humanity and God is dissolved into a pantheistic soup. Wherever religion tempts people to deny and disobey revelation, religion becomes an act of idolatry. But there is hope for religion because it represents human possibility at the highest level if it is redeemed. The good news is that in the same manner in which human beings may be justified and sanctified, so, too, can their religion. When religion is separated from God, it can become the basis for sin. However, in the hand of God, religion may become the context for revelation. Religion may be used by God, and so religious experience may become the servant of revelation. In *Christian*

Dogmatics, Barth goes beyond *Romans* in which there was a rejection of religion within the divine economy. Here religion may also signify a relationship with God.

Christian Dogmatics did not achieve what Barth had set out to accomplish. Some years before he set out to rewrite his commentary on *Romans* and now a similar challenge faced him, because *Christian Dogmatics* was unable to relate the self-revelation of God to history and somehow not compromise the divine revelation. The new challenge facing Barth was how he could use categories such as faith, experience, belief, and the knowledge of God and not make them an independent basis for theology. How could God be the proper basis for theology and at the same time not compromise the human as participant in the act of faith? The way was not yet clear to Barth.

The hermeneutical key that Barth sought was at last found when in the summer of 1930 he prepared a seminar on Anselm's *Cur Deus Homo.* This was the occasion of Barth's book *Anselm: Fides Quaerens Intellectum.* Barth began to understand theology as faith's search for understanding. In spite of failures or accomplishments in understanding, faith remains faith. And yet, as will be seen, faith has a certain kind of understanding, or we may say a certain kind of knowledge. Faith's understanding or faith's knowledge is truth. This is the direct object of faith and that which makes theology possible. There are some limits the theologian must keep in mind regarding the theological task.

Of first importance is the recognition that any meaningful understanding of faith that occurs within the church is tied to the church's confession of faith. The challenge that faith presents within the church is not merely the need to contemplate truth but also to rethink the truth of the confession. Truth is both the ground and the goal of theology.

So we may go a step further and acknowledge that theology has to do more than meditate on the truth on which faith is based. The theological task is to investigate the nature of the truth believed. However, the theologian is not free to postulate any view of truth that is appealing to him or her. Truth is given in the birth of the community of faith. It is this truth given in the confession that must be the point of departure for the theological task. As the theologian investigates the nature of truth given in the confession, he/she discovers that truth is more than an opinion: it points to the mystery of God and the miracle of faith.

The provisional nature of theological statements must be noted. Theological statements as such are not final or complete. This is so because all our statements concerning God are inadequate. Our ways of understanding are not God's ways. It is only God who can speak for God. And yet Barth insists that in spite of these shortcomings, a genuine knowledge of God is possible. This is because Christian faith presents us with symbols and objects of knowledge that provide a basis for knowledge. These symbols and objects of knowledge are like a mirror in which we may look at the likeness of God. Although we see God's face in the mirror, we should not believe that the mirror is God's face. And yet in the mirror we see God's face, which more or less corresponds to the truth. Yet what we have is inadequate, because it is a reflection of God and not God. It begins to become clear that theological statements do not have certainty as faith statements. The theologian should not speak as if his or her statements have the authority of the truth. On the contrary, such statements will be judged by the truth. Therefore, the theologian must keep in mind the provisional nature of his or her findings and that to a certain extent this work is experimental. For this reason, theology should not merely accept criticism but should invite it. But what if the theologian cites Scripture to substantiate his or her work? Citing Scripture is not yet theology—theology begins where this ends.

Consequently, claims Barth, there is no perfect theology. It's never a completed achievement. Truths that have been hidden will yet be revealed. So even in the presence of the great theologians of the church, one is undaunted because one has the possibility of going beyond them.

But then if we are invited to do theology and to go beyond

Anselm, Aquinas, and Augustine, how may we be sure that our theology represents progress? What is normative here? It is the struggle at this level that makes theology a very vulnerable science. Here an appeal has to be made to Scripture, which is not only the source of faith's understanding but the criterion by which new departures are to be judged. If these new departures do not contradict the teaching of Scripture, they are to be allowed as valid.

Theology must not be construed as a purely intellectual enterprise. It comes from faith and is throughout powered and motivated by faith. A false faith or an absence of faith can wreak havoc in the attempt to do theology. The theologian is required to have a unique faith that moves toward its unique object. This faith must be nourished by Scripture.

Because theology is faith seeking understanding, it stands to reason that prayer has a unique role, since prayer is both the exercise and the practice of faith. Truth, which is the object of theology, cannot be realized with one's own intellectual powers unaided by God's grace. This grace is made possible through prayer. But in prayer we discover that what God gives is not so much gifts, but God gives Godself. Therefore the understanding that faith seeks is the knowledge of God and not merely knowledge about God. It is the very presence of God that constitutes the basis for the truth that is the object of theology. Faith prays for understanding as it seeks understanding. The key here has to do with faith's relationship to its object. One's piety or sincerity does not determine the object. On the contrary faith is made faith by the truth of its object. Faith is created by its object.

Both faith and understanding are human activities, and they derive from their object that God is our savior in Jesus Christ and that God gives Godself to be known. This is the main reason why theology may not be based on faith's piety or sincerity. Faith alone cannot inform us concerning the object of faith.

It is precisely at this point that the theological task has to be differentiated from the philosophical task. The theologian cannot allow philosophical presuppositions to be the controlling motif for the object of theology.

Faith then is not the starting point of theology. It is the object of theology that faith seeks to understand. The object of theology is God, and it is God that is the starting point of theology. However, as it has been suggested earlier, we cannot know God as God is in Godself, because God dwells in light inaccessible. But God who is great in mercy has revealed Godself in the life, death, and resurrection of Jesus Christ. Apart from Jesus Christ, God is unknown and unknowable.

The first principle in theological method is that theology is oriented toward God. God is the object of faith. God has revealed Godself in Jesus Christ. This calls attention to the second principle of theological method that theology must be oriented toward Jesus Christ. This is so, contends Barth, because Jesus Christ is the object of faith and faith's understanding. But the Jesus Christ who is the object of faith is not Jesus Christ as a principle but the Jesus whose life and history are narrated in Scripture. This history to which Scripture calls attention is not merely the history of a man but of the God-man who sets forth in his life, death, and resurrection the revelation of the incomprehensible God. The witness of the Bible is not merely a biography of Jesus Christ but a confession of faith in him. The biblical writers believed in him not merely through their intellect, but because they were illumined by the presence of the Holy Spirit. So for Barth, the Bible is understood in two lights. The Bible is understood as an historical document, and as such it is open all along the line for investigation as a document. But the Bible is also understood as a believing witness to God's self-revelation manifested in Jesus Christ. This means that theology also ought to orient itself toward Scripture, that is, toward the believing witness of the Bible.

We come to a faith that seeks to understand. It is faith in the incomprehensible God who has revealed Godself in Jesus Christ as is attested to by the believing witness of the Scriptures.

The relationship between God and the creature cannot be one of equality, to posit a relationship of equality would simply mean that God had ceased being God and that human beings were elevated to the status of God. And yet the relationship cannot be totally dissimilar either or that would indicate that human beings cannot know God. The way between these two extremes Barth refers to as analogy. This middle path is not to be understood as one of partial identity and partial dissimilarity. The truth is that creation is similar to God in every way that it is dissimilar. Because of sin, our concepts and words cannot claim God as their object, but God may, in spite of us, claim to be the true object of the words. Through God's revelatory act, the process and fact of analogy is established from above. This means that the ultimate basis for analogy is God's grace revealed in God's son, Jesus Christ. Although creator and creature are unequal, God is immanent in God's creation, and God loves God's world. Therefore talk about God must not only affirm God's transcendence but also God's immanence. God is present to the world God has created. God sustains and controls the world without taking away human freedom. Because God is present to this world, we cannot talk about God's enmity or alienation from the world.

INSIGHTS AND VISTAS FOR THEOLOGICAL METHOD

Barth specifically underscores some of the primary ingredients in theological method:

The question of truth, with which theology is throughout concerned is the question as to the agreement between the language about God peculiar to the Church and the essence of the Church. The criterion of Christian language in the past and future as well as in the present time, is the essence of the Church, which is Jesus Christ, God in his gracious approach to man in revelation and reconciliation. Has Christian language its source in him? Does it lead to him? None of these questions can be put without the others, but each in all its force must be put independently.[5]

There are a number of insights to which we must pay particular attention in the passage cited above. The first has to do with the church's role in the task of theology. Hans Urs von Balthasar illuminates Barth's attempt to relate the Word of God to the church: "The Word of God becomes a 'happening' in the Church, and the Church makes this Word the alpha and omega; it becomes the primary legislation event, governing all other sets of first principles."[6] For Barth, theology is a function of the church: "The Church tests herself by essaying dogmatics. To the Church is given the promise of the criterion for Christian faith, namely the revelation of God. The Church can ply dogmatics. Even in the Church dogmatics need not be the work of a special theological science. Yet dogmatics is impossible outside the Church."[7] To be in the church is to be called upon with others by Jesus Christ. Here the Christological nature of the church is evident.

But this raises the whole question of the place of reason in doing theology. It is quite clear that this discussion between human reason and the revelation attested to in the church provides the very basis of theology. So theology becomes a discussion between human reason and divine revelation. It is import that this discussion takes place within the church and not outside it. The church ceases to be the church if it presumes that through the exercise of human reason it can attain the knowledge of divine revelation.

According to Barth, the epistemological question cannot be, how is human knowledge of revelation possible? This assumes that revelation may be deduced from an empirical investigation of human knowledge. Rather, the appropriate question is, what is the real basis of the human understanding of revelation? In answering this question, Barth insists that we must begin at the beginning and not that it is revelation in the first place that creates the point of contact between people and God. This means then that we must look to revelation and not to human reason in an attempt to answer this question. To locate the point of contact in human reason is to abandon the theological task and seek the answer outside the church.

The focus on the primacy of revelation in providing the nexus between humanity and God prevents theology from being reduced to anthropology. To allow for an anthropological point of departure in preference to a Christological one not only would call attention to the temptation of theology being reduced to anthropology but would focus on an important distinction between theology and the philosophy of religion. In the practice of philosophy of religion, the philosopher is not restricted to practice in his/her community. The philosopher may choose to practice outside of that community or to follow the research wherever it may lead. Philosophy of religion may be the reflection of an individual in the solitude of his/her ivory tower. Or it may represent the attempt through reason and logic to reach God. This is the very opposite of the theological task and would call into question the ecclesiastical character of theology.

The theologian is accountable to the church and seeks truth that is already given in the birth of that community. If theology is regarded as a science like psychology and philosophy, we immediately highlight the human effort and in so doing we minimize the centrality of divine revelation. The problem here is that what would determine the basis and the content of God-talk would not be the revelation of God as received in church but human revelation. The careful student, however, should note the dialectical tension that Barth maintains throughout his work. Although he refuses to allow reason to be the point of departure for the theological task, reason nonetheless has an important role in doing theology. He writes:

> By designating itself a "science," theology brings itself into line; as a human effort after truth, it confesses its solidarity with other efforts of this kind which today are united for good and all under this idea; enters a protest against the conception that it is raised ontologically above these others . . . and reminds itself of the fact that it is only a "science," and so of the "profaneness" with which it too, on its relatively special path, does its work even in the most exalted regions.[8]

Barth points out that there are two types of theology. There are what he calls regular, or scientific, theology and irregular, or unscientific, theology. According to Barth, regular theology is what should occur in a good theological school, and it has in common with other sciences the quest for knowledge. It is in relation to the church, however, that theology spells out its understanding of what is scientific rather than allow any other discipline to impose on it. This is so because truth is given within the church, and it is within the church that theology may be judged.

Regular theology must impress upon the student how one question breaks up into many questions, and how these many questions are open all along the line from every possible point of view and are all interrelated. A regular, or school, theology must, therefore, cover the whole range of concepts and themes of significance for church proclamation regarding the biblical testimony on which this proclamation has its concrete criterion and its bearing on the history of dogma and theology.

Although Barth is not yet saying that church history or the history of proclamation should be sources for doing theology on the same level as proclamation, Scripture, and revelation, he is stating that scientific theology does not dare ignore church history, or for that matter, the *sitz im leben*. Here then, theology attains a level of sophistication that is to be differentiated from irregular dogmatics. It is of first importance that the church has regular dogmatics.

On the other hand, irregular theology lacks the consistency with which dogmatics functions in relationship to church proclamation, the history of dogma, and Scripture. Barth cites Athanasius and Luther as theologians who practice irregular dogmatics. Had Barth been familiar with Martin Luther King Jr.'s approach to theology, I believe he would have included him in this category.

For Barth, the marks of a good theology are: (1) It must be busy with the testing of church proclamation to see if it is in harmony with the revelation attested to in Scripture; (2) theology must be busy with the criticism and revision of church proclamation and not merely with a repetitive exposition of it. The criterion of good theology is the revelation attested to in Scripture. Good theology must be scriptural.

We must now look at Barth's claim that the essence of the

church is the norm and ground of the theological task. Barth writes: "It is from the direction of Jesus Christ as the essence of the Church that we may expect free personal decision as to what ought to be the proper content of Christian language, and so also as to what should be the way to knowledge of dogma."9 The Word of God is the standard by which church proclamation and church dogmatics are to be measured. We experience the Word of God as language, mystery, and act; language, mystery and act, in turn, are centered in the same truth that reveals God as Father, Son, and Holy Spirit.

When Barth speaks of the Word of God, he is quite specifically referring to Jesus Christ. The Word of God encounters us in proclamation, Scripture and revelation. It is in these three ways that the Word of God is known. The Word of God encounters humanity as language. It is one mind communicating with another mind. God's Word means God speaks. There is a correspondence of God's language and human language. For all its distinctiveness, the Word of God is rational, natural, personally spoken, and directed. It is timely and historical. Yet for all its similarities, it is unique; it is simultaneously true and real. The Word of God is not bound, it is free. The church has received the Word and is commissioned to proclaim it. Proclamation takes place with the claim and expectation that it is "human language in and through which God speaks, like a king through the mouth of his herald."10 By proclamation, Barth essentially means preaching and sacrament. It is in preaching and sacrament that the commission to serve God's word is realized.

Preaching remembers and expects Jesus Christ, announcing God's promise to be present. The sacrament remembers and expects Jesus Christ in action. Both preaching and sacrament are based solely on God's promise and presence. Proclamation as the speaking and hearing of God's language goes on at the direction of God. Its motivation is not human desire. Proclamation should not be an attempt to describe and expound personal convictions. Preaching takes place because God orders it. Therefore it is not based upon human but divine will.

Obedience to the Word of God for proclamation means obedience to the revelation attested to in the human words of Holy Scriptures. Barth is immensely impressed with the holiness of Scripture. The authority of the Bible is similar to the distinctive claim of church proclamation. It is from time to time that the human words of Scripture become the event of the Word of God. Regarding the question of authority, Scripture and church proclamation must be carefully distinguished from each other. Scripture is spoken to and for the church in such a way thatit stands as the norm and criterion of the church's words. Barth puts it this way:

> *In this same phenomenal likeness is next to be found also the unlikeness in order between Holy Scripture and proclamation to-day, the superiority, the purely constitutive significance of the former for the latter, the restrictedness of the reality of proclamation to-day by its foundation upon Holy Scripture and by its obligations to it—therefore, the fundamental distinction of the written word of the prophets and apostles above all other human words later in the Church and needing to be spoken to-day.[11]*

The Bible is not a history of the church's conversation with itself. Given to the church, Scripture is the original witness of the prophets and apostles to God's revelation. It confronts the church in such a way as to remain over against it. The canon is regulative because of its own imposition upon the church rather than because of any decision the church made. The Word is the mother of the church. The authority of Scripture comes on the basis of God's decision to speak God's Word, in the words of the Bible. In a real sense, our talk about God must be guided by an exposition of the Old and New Testaments. God has located God's language to people in the language of the prophets and apostles and in the revelation to which they attest.

For Barth, the words of Scripture are not intrinsically the Word of God. There is no intrinsic connection between God's language and the language of the Bible. The power of the biblical word has to do with the miracle of its witness to divine revelation. It is in this sense that Barth approaches the hermeneutical question of the relationship between divine content and human form: God's Word and human words in Scripture. In interpreting Scripture, Barth insists that God's Word should clarify, communicate, and interpret itself in the particular human words its has chosen. As human words, biblical words do not speak of themselves but of divine revelation to which they witness. This places in focus the relationship between the text and its subject in the interpretive task. All human language exists not for itself but for the sake of its subject matter and language is only language so far as the subject matter is communicated.

The understanding of the human language of the Bible means perceiving the subject matter, revelation. Hearing the biblical Word means hearing the biblical content not apart from but in human form. When the event of the Word takes place, human language truly becomes language; its words take on full meaning as human words when the divine content discloses itself.

It cannot be emphasized too strongly that for Barth, Scripture is not to be confused with the revelation to which it attests. Scripture, like proclamation, is the Word of God in a definitive but contingent way. It is definitive as the original witness to the revelation of God in Jesus Christ. It is contingent as God decides from time to time to effect God's Word in the words of the Bible. The Holy Scripture and proclamation are witnesses to revelation. Therefore revelation is a third form of the Word of God. Whereas Scripture and proclamation become the Word of God from time to time, revelation is God's Word being so in itself. Barth states clearly:

Thus we must think of every state of revelation as a process of revelation, that is, as conditioned by the very act of revelation; of every happening in which revelation takes place as connected with what in this act happens once for all; of all fulfilled time as fulfilled by the fullness of this time. But revelation itself is connected with nothing different or higher or earlier than itself. Revelation as such is not relative. Revelation, in fact, does not differ from the Person of Jesus Christ, and again does not differ from the reconciliation that took place in him. To say revelation is to say, "The Word became flesh." [12]

Despite the differentiation of Scripture, proclamation, and revelation, Barth affirms that they cannot be separated from each other: "It is one and the same, whether we regard it as revelation, as the Bible, or as proclamation. There is no distinction of degree of value between these three forms."[13]

Unlike human language, God's language does exist for its own sake. God's language does not point away from itself toward revelation but is identical with revelation. Analogically, Barth relates revelation both to the Word of God and to the Trinity. Trinitarian theology, as Barth understands it, is the revelatory answer to a constellation of questions that ask after the subject, the content, and the effect of revelation. The theology of the Trinity emphasized that God as the one who does the revealing is identical with what is revealed and how revelation happens. For Barth, God's nature as Revealer, Revelation, and Revealedness corresponds to Father, Son, and Holy Spirit: "Revelation in the Bible does not mean a minus, a something other over against God. It means the equal of God, a repetition of God. . . . Thus, it is God Himself, it is the same God in unimpaired unity, who according to the Bible's understanding of revelation is the revealing God, and the event of revelation, and its effect upon man."[14]

Revelation tells of the sovereignty of God as Father, Son, and Holy Spirit. In God's unveiling of Godself, God takes form. God speaks a word, God is present in God's Son, Jesus of Nazareth. God makes Godself known doing what human beings cannot do for themselves. People cannot speak for God or make God known. God speaks for Godself. God becomes what God is not. God becomes manifest. This happens as God distinguishes Godself from Godself revealing God as Son and as Lord. Yet in the distinguishing, God remains God. There is no loss to God or curtailing of God's freedom and mystery. God does not give Godself away, for the form of God's appearing is a concealing one. Barth writes cogently:

*It is the concept of form which we must single out from
what has been said as the decisive one. Whoever and
whatever the self-revealing God may be otherwise, this is
certain that in his revelation, according to the witness of the
Bible, He takes form, and that this taking form is His self-
unveiling. For Him it is not impossible and for Him it is not
too petty a thing, to be his own double in His revelation,
double so far as His self-unveiling, His taking form is
obviously not a thing that goes without saying but an event,
and an event at that which can be explained by or derived
from neither the will and act of man.*[15]

The event of revelation, whereby the self-revealing God in his
unrevealing form becomes known to certain people, is also an act of
God's lordship. The act of disclosure of God as Father and Son at
particular times and places in history is the result of the activity of
the Holy Spirit. The very fact that this revelation can be spoken of
calls attention to the activity of the Holy Spirit in history, impinging
on human existence in the self-revelation of God as Father and Son.
Because of this, God remains Lord of his revelation in that not only
is God the one who is revealed and the one who remains hidden but
God is the one who does and accomplishes the revelation: "God
reveals Himself as the Spirit, not as any spirit, not as the discover-
able and arousable subsoil of man's spiritual life, but as the Spirit of
the Father and the Son, and as the same one God."[16]

God is the one and the same in all respects. The trinitarian
exposition of God is congenial with Barth's understanding of the
Word of God because concreteness, mystery, history, and contingency are all implied in the notion of God as speaker and triune. The
notion of the Word of God as God's language is not set aside when
Barth discusses the existence of the Word in Jesus of Nazareth. In
Jesus of Nazareth it is God's word that is incarnate. The incarnation
is a concrete event, for it is the existence of God in a particular
history and in a definite time in the unique person of Jesus Christ.
This temporality and historicity of revelation cannot be explained

away; it can only be recognized and acknowledged. We may speak of a Christological focus in Karl Barth's theology. It is this focus that provides the main key to understanding the doctrines of creation, reconciliation, redemption, and the nature and destiny of humanity. Because God has made Godself known in Jesus Christ in a definitive way, it is ungrateful for us to seek God in nature, in history, or in religion. Jesus Christ is normative of our knowledge of God and therefore stands in judgment on all other forms of the knowledge of God. There is no highway from people to God, but rather a clear way from God to humanity, and Jesus Christ is the way. This was demonstrated for us in the incarnation when God became human.

Hence, the appropriate starting point of theology is the Word of God revealed in Jesus Christ. This certainly is one reason why Barth rejects the Roman Catholic doctrine of *analogia entis* and natural theology. To move theologically from a consideration about humanity to a consideration of God is to blur the relationship between creature/creation and God. The *analogia entis* must become *analogia fidei*. The bottom line is the danger of beginning with humanity rather than with God.

BARTH AND KING

It is satisfying to learn that in his only visit to the United States in 1963, Karl Barth had a meeting with Martin Luther King Jr.[17] Yet it is disappointing that all Barth says about the visit with King was that together they took a photograph before a church. Martin Luther King Jr. does not mention the visit, and so we do not have any way of judging what they talked about or knowing if, in fact, they talked about any theological issues.

The year 1963 was extremely busy for Martin Luther King Jr., a watershed in the life of the movement he led. *Time* magazine made him their Man of the Year. The march on Washington had placed the race issue on the front burner of the American agenda. The great success of the march provided a much needed respite for King and his colleagues. Then he had to deal with the bombing of the Sixteenth Street Baptist Church in Birmingham in which four girls were killed. This was also the year President John F. Kennedy was killed, and King became increasingly convinced that he would be killed in similar fashion. There were also the disappointments of St. Augustine and Birmingham, but toward the end of the year was the announcement that King had been elected to receive the Nobel Peace Prize. Throughout all of this, King made dozens of speeches all over the country.

Karl Barth's trip to the United States that year was also tightly scheduled. He visited ten states in seven weeks and gave many lectures and interviews. It is no wonder that perhaps all he and King had time for was a friendly smile and handshake, coupled with a photograph. We are fortunate that King shared with us some of his views concerning Barth's work both in his articles and term papers written for Boston University. Before we look at King's assessment of Barth's theology, however, it may be well for us to look at some points of convergence and divergence between their two approaches to theology.

The main difference between Barth's and King's approaches to the theological task is tantamount to the difference between Tillich's and Barth's approaches. The difference has to do with the point of departure. We may recall earlier in this chapter that Barth mentions the importance of the pastor-theologian having the Bible in one hand and the newspaper in the other. Further, throughout this chapter we note the passionate involvement of Barth's theology with people in an attempt to mediate God's grace. Barth's theology could also be considered a covenantal theology, a theology that takes the divine/human encounter seriously. Or we could say that in Barth's approach to theology we have the broad strokes of a theology of correlation.

The main difference between Barth's and Tillich's approaches parallels the distinctions between Barth and King. Whereas Tillich and King begin with the existential pole of the correlation, Barth begins with the message of the Word of God. Tillich and King begin with the questions that arise from the situation, but Barth begins with the answer. It is the point of departure that determines the focus and character of Barth's theology. The starting point for Barth is not the questions we bring but the fact that we are questioned by God. God questions us: "Adam where are you?" "Cain, where is your brother?" Or Jesus asks, "Who do you say that I am?"

Barth is concerned that if we allow societal issues such as poverty or discrimination or economic exploitation to frame the question, then we begin at the wrong pole. We begin on the outside rather than on the inside. We begin with people rather than with God. It is the Word of God that is the subject matter of theology and not the word of people. The Word of God made known in creation, reconciliation, and redemption. So for Barth, we must begin by seeing ourselves in the light of the Word of God. When we see ourselves in the light of the Word of God, we see ourselves as creatures, God's pardoned sinners, and God's future redeemed. Humanity is understood eschatologically—that is, in the light of the Lordship of Christ. To begin with the answer rather than the question is to avoid the danger of beginning with the wrong analysis. For Barth, the gospel provides an appropriate point of departure for talk about God, humanity, and the world in each and every generation and situation.

But King would counter that because theology has to begin with the existential situation; theology is not free of risks, and one of the risks is that of a wrong analysis. This may be unavoidable sometimes, because theology is a human enterprise. God does not do theology. It is people who do theology. Therefore, King begins his theological reflection at the point of human existence. He begins with an analysis of a particular moral problem and often goes on to indicate what loyalty to Christian faith or to Jesus Christ entails. The attempt to allow human experience to be the starting point of theological reflection allows King to take seriously the complexity of the existential situation and at the same time minimize distortions as he moves to other frames of reference. But because King is more of an irregular theologian than a scientific theologian (to use Karl Barth's phrase), there are times when existential questions are raised under the impact of the answer. An examination of his sermons and speeches as a clue to his approach indicates that for him there is more than one approach to the theological task, but as a rule of thumb he begins with the situation. With a firm belief in the moral law at work in the universe and a confidence and conviction in some notion of prevenient grace that suffuses all of existence, King contends that to allow a description of human experience to be the starting point of theology is not antithetical to Christian faith and belief, even though the analysis is not derived directly from Scripture or divine revelation.

There are two illustrations of King's approach to the theological task that highlight this:

An understanding of the "finite freedom" of man is one of the contributions of existentialism, and its perception of the anxiety and conflict produced in man's personal and social life by the perilous and ambiguous structure of existence is especially meaningful for our time. A common denominator in atheistic or theistic existentialism is that man's existential situation is estranged from his essential nature. . . . While the ultimate Christian answer is not found in any of these existential assertions, there is much here by which the theologian may describe the true state of man's existence.[18]

Or again, in an attempt to get at an analysis of the structures of oppression coupled with an eschatological vision of what God requires even in a situation of oppression, King states:

The misuse of capitalism may also lead to tragic exploitation. This has so often happened in your nation. I am told that one-tenth of 1 percent of the population controls more than 40 percent of the wealth. America, how often have you taken necessities from the masses and given luxuries to the classes. If you are to be a truly Christian nation, you must solve this problem. . . . You must use your powerful economic resources to eliminate poverty on earth. God never intended one people to live in superfluous and

inordinate wealth, while others know only deadening
poverty. God wants all his children to have the basic
necessities of life, and he has left the universe "enough and
to spare" for that purpose.[19]

Here King is interested in relating God-talk to the politics of
oppression and injustice. There is a theological commitment on
King's part to change the conditions in the society that crush the
poor and those edged out of the mainstream of American life. This
commitment leads to action on behalf of the victims and in solidarity
with victims to create a new order, a reconciled and restored order in
which the dignity and humanity of all of God's children can be
affirmed. But this new restored and reconciled order must pass
through struggle. No struggle, no victory.

Now we must look more closely at King's conversation with
Barth. In his essay "Pilgrimage to Nonviolence," King writes: "Niebuhr's great contribution to contemporary theology is that he refused
the false optimism characteristic of a great segment of Protestant
liberalism, without falling into the anti-rationalism of the continental
theologian Karl Barth."[20] In this essay, King contends that in its
attempt to preserve the transcendence of God and correct liberalism's optimism regarding human nature, neo-orthodoxy went too far
in being pessimistic about human nature and in "stressing a God
who was hidden, unknown, and 'wholly other': "In its revolt against
overemphasis on the power of reason in liberalism, Neo-orthodoxy
fell into a mood of antirationalism and semifundamentalism, stressing a narrow uncritical biblicism. This approach, I felt, was inadequate both for the church and for personal life."[21]

King's difficulties with Barth's approach to theology reside at
two levels. The first concerns Barth's view of human nature; the
second concerns Barth's doctrine of God, which he spells out in a
graduate paper written for Boston University.[22] There are three areas
in which King criticizes Barth's conception of God: (a) the transcendent God, (b) the unknown God and (c) the revelation of God in
Jesus Christ.

On the question of the transcendence of God, King points out that Barth alludes to the "infinite qualitative distinction" between God and God's world: "Barth's God is 'above us, above space and time, and above all concepts and opinions and all potentialities.'"[23] God is the "Wholly other." The implications are twofold, King argues. (1) It means that we cannot discover God through the study of humanity; there is no path from human beings to God. (2) Barth rejects a *theologia naturalis;* we do not find God in natural theology. The good news is that through the babe of Bethlehem and through the cross of Calvary, God has broken into history in saving knowledge.

On the question of the Unknown God, King alludes to mystery being for Barth the meaning of God. "The hidden God remains hidden," writes King, "even when God reveals Godself." Finding a link with Barth, King cites him with approval: "Barth writes: 'God is personal, but personal in an incomprehensible way, insofar as the conception of his personality surpasses all our views of personality."[24] Even the knowledge that comes through faith is a knowledge that acknowledges the majesty and the mystery of God and hence is incomplete. The finite is not capable of the infinite. Even when God reveals Godself to human beings, God is even further away.

But King reminds us that to get at what Barth has in mind, we ought to be sensitive to Barth's dialectical method, which is clothed in paradox. The language of Barth's dialectical method is paradox. States King: "Barth uses the procedure of the examination room where questions are put requiring answers. The answer contains the question and the question implies the answer. . . . often the no is but a concealed yes."[25] The way out of paradox is in God. It is human error to seek the answer in time or on earth.

Finally, King gives an exposition of Barth's view of the revelation of God in Jesus Christ. King points out that although for Barth there is no way from humanity to God, there is a way from God to humanity. It is in Christ crucified and risen that God offers a bridge between heaven and earth. King summarizes Barth's views:

It is in him that the impossibilities are combined, the
irreconcilables are here reconciled: God and man, eternity
and time, death and resurrection. Here in him, the conflict is
somehow resolved and we are saved.[26]

King instructs us that for Barth, Jesus Christ is the answer to
the problems raised by the transcendence of God, the brokenness of
humanity, and the unknowability of God. This theology, states King,
begins upward and downward, rather than outward from the collec-
tive experience of action and ministry.

Although many contemporary liberationists dismiss Barth's
neo-orthodoxy, it must be acknowledged that Barth has had a profound impact on the most influential Black theologian today in
North America: James Cone. We now turn to Cone's thought and its
relationship to the theology of Martin Luther King Jr.

CHAPTER 4 — JAMES CONE'S PERSPECTIVE

James Cone wrote his dissertation at Northwestern University on Karl Barth's anthropology, and Barth's influence is unmistakable in Cone's formulation of the theological task. The centrality of Christology in Cone's theology, the confessional nature of his theology, and the plea for liberation in the community of the oppressed all point from time to time to Barth's hand in the background. Alluding to the Christological focus of his work, Cone states:

> *Christian theology begins and ends with Jesus Christ. He is the point of departure for everything to be said about God, man, and the world. That is why Christology is the starting point of Karl Barth's* Dogmatics . . . . *To speak of the Christian gospel is to speak of Christ who is the content of its message and without whom Christianity ceases to be. Therefore the answer to the question "What is Christianity?" can be given in two words: Jesus Christ.*[1]

The broad strokes of Paul Tillich's method are also at work in Cone's approach to the theological task.[2] The important factor, however, is that Cone goes much further than both Barth and Tillich in giving specificity and social concreteness to his understanding of theology. This appears to be one of the burdens of Cone's later work, that of allowing the Black experience to provide the very basis for articulating God's encounter with humanity.

For Barth and Tillich, Black and third world people were invisible. The struggles of these people did not provide an agenda for their theology. This was especially true of Tillich, who lived in Harlem yet did not allow the tragedy in Black life to find a place in his theology. It is painful to recall that Paul Tillich lived and worked in the United States during the civil rights era yet did not comment on the injustices of all sorts ravaging Black life. Karl Barth was just as silent.

Issues that are unimportant to Barth and Tillich become the center of theological attention for Cone. Cone was able to go further than Tillich and Barth not only because of his sensitivity to the plight of oppressed people but also because of his rootedness in the Black church. The role of the Black church in the development of Black theology reached a high point in two significant movements that emerged in the 1950s and 1960s in North America: the civil rights movement, led by Martin Luther King Jr., and the Black power movement, led by Stokely Carmichael and Malcolm X. The Black power movement is related to the Black church not only because the term *Black power* was coined at a rally in Chicago in May 1965 by a Baptist pastor from Harlem, Adam Clayton Powell, but also because of its philosophy of Black dignity and Black self-determination. Further, the philosophy of Black power has its roots in the teaching of Black church leaders such as Nat Turner, Denmark Vesey, Bishop Henry McNeil Turner, and Marcus Garvey.

The civil rights movement and the Black power movement went in different directions. The civil rights movement aimed at a reformation of American life, and the Black power movement demanded change in the structures of oppression. Each in significant ways had immense influence upon the development and articulation of Black theology.

In the midst of the Black power struggle, which came to a head with the issuance of James Foreman's Black manifesto to the white religious establishment, Cone, a little-known theologian, published his first book, *Black Theology and Black Power.* In this book, Cone contends that Black power is the power of Jesus Christ: "The existence of *the* Church is grounded exclusively in Christ. And in twentieth century America, *Christ means Black Power!*"[3]

In the chapter "Black Church and Black Power," Cone argues that his understanding of Black power is not strange to the Black church but rather emerged from its life and teaching. While grounding his work in the Black power movement, and at the same time calling into question the love ethic of the civil rights movement, Cone writes:

> *Some black preachers, like the Rev. Highland Garnet, even urged outright rebellion against the evils of white power. He knew that appeals to "love" or "goodwill" would have little effects on minds warped by their own high estimation of themselves. Therefore, he taught that the spirit of liberty is a gift from God, and God thus endows the slave with the zeal to break the chains of slavery.*[4]

Further, Cone states that the Black power movement emerged out of the civil rights movement, because Black people had become disenchanted with Martin King's demand to love the enemy.

ENDURING THEMES

There are a number of themes that emerge in Dr. Cone's first book, *Black Theology and Black Power,* that endure as Cone's vision of Black theology expands: first, the dialogue between white theology and Black existence; second, Cone's insistence that Black theology is a church discipline; and third, the indissoluble connection between theology and ethics.

A cursory look at the index of *Black Theology and Black Power* reveals Cone demonstrating his competence in white theology, with incisive and insightful discussions of scholars as diverse as Emil Brunner, Rudolf Bultmann, Dietrich Bonhoeffer, Günther Bornkamm, Billy Graham, Karl Jasper, Sören Kierkegaard, and Richard Niebuhr, to name a few. This should not surprise us as Cone mentions that both his college and seminary education were steeped in the writings of white philosophers and theologians. Cone writes:

> *Like most college and seminary students of my*
> *generation, I faithfully studied philosophy and theology—*
> *from the pre-socratics to modern existentialism and*
> *linguistic analysis, from Justin Martyr, Irenaeus, and Origen*
> *to Karl Barth, Bultmann, and Tillich. I was an expert on*
> *Karl Barth and knew well, the theological issues that shaped*
> *his theology. I wrote papers in seminary on the Barth and*
> *Brunner debates, the knowledge of God in contemporary*
> *theology, Bultmann's program of demythologization, the*
> *Tillichian doctrine of God as being itself, and concluded my*
> *formal education with a Ph.D dissertation on Barth's*
> *anthropology.[5]*

It was highly improbable that Cone would engage in theological analysis of the Black experience without reference to these theologians that he encountered in seminary and graduate school. Further, because he knew the theologians of the white church very well, this gave him ready access to criticism of the white church and its theology, which Cone furthers: "For the sickness of the Church in America is intimately involved with the bankruptcy of American Theology. When the Church fails to live up to its appointed mission, it means that theology is partly responsible. Therefore, it is impossible to criticize the Church and its lack of relevancy without criticizing theology for its failure to perform its function."[6]

Cone indicates that the central problem with American theology is its attempt to affirm and confirm the language of unreality in the church, rather than call the church to its central task of acting out the Gospel. Theology, if it is to save its own soul, must be related to life. That is, the central problems of the society must become grist for the theological mill. According to Cone, a rereading of Barth's *Dogmatics* would make this observation clear, because the revolution that Barth led in the theological arena took place in Hitler's

Germany and reflected the political, economic, and social problems of that society.

If American theology were to learn from Karl Barth, it would take the sociopolitical context of theology seriously. This means, among other things, that the way white people do theology would have to change. They could not continue to theologize as if Black people are invisible. The white church could not continue to exclude Black people from its worship services. For the white church/ theology to continue its exclusionary practice makes it run the risk of losing its own soul. Cone highlights for us a normative vision of the church:

> *If the real Church is the people of God, whose primary task is that of being Christ to the world by proclaiming the message of the gospel (kerygma,) by rendering services of liberation (diakonia,) and by being itself a manifestation of the nature of the new society (kononia,) then the empirical institutionalized white church has failed on all counts. It certainly has not rendered services of liberation to the poor. Rather, it illustrates the values of a sick society which oppresses the poor.[7]*

Here Cone refuses to be indifferent to or to ignore the white church.

Cecil Wayne Cone suggests that in the early years, Cone is an angry young radical fired by an ethic of Black power who lashes out at white people as he indicates that what Black people want and demand is liberation "by any means necessary." Cecil Cone writes:

> *Because of the tone of his writings, Cone came across at first as merely a young, militant black caught "on the fence between the Christian faith and the religion of Black power." Yet when one takes the time to scrutinize carefully Cone's effort in his first book, there slowly emerges a deeper attempt at a theology of Black Power.[8]*

A deeper look at Cone's work also indicates the forging of a dialogue, albeit a difficult dialogue, with white theology and the white church. Cone challenges the white church and its theology to take sides with the oppressed. The white church is urged to become Black and its theologians revolutionary and Christian.

Implicit in this difficult dialogue with the white church and its theology is a call to repentance and reconciliation, which, however, is not merely an invitation for a change of heart. The invitation is also for change in economics and politics. Change is also required in the social situation. This radical *metanoia* is represented in the call and invitation to become Black. Cone writes:

Therefore, God's Word of reconciliation means that we can only be justified by becoming black. Reconciliation makes us all black. Through this radical change, we become identified totally with the suffering of the black masses. It is this fact that makes all white churches anti-christian in their essence. To be Christian is to be one of those whom God has chosen. God has chosen black people. It is to be expected that many white people will ask: "How can I a white *man become black? My skin is white and there is nothing I can do." Being black in America has very little to do with skin color. To be black means that your heart, your soul, your mind, and your body are where the dispossessed are.[9]*

Here, Cone hints at the double use of the category blackness, and is intentionally ambiguous in its use. Blackness, on the one hand, provides the content of liberation as Black people are called to true humanity, respect, and the dignity of self-determination. On the other hand, Blackness also points to what white people are called to become.

In the attempt to relate the category blackness to the Black as well as the white community Cone makes a number of moves. Although his theology owes its genesis to the left wing of the civil rights movement, one may also see the hand of Martin Luther King Jr. in the background from time to time. The press for reconciliation is a direct influence of the life and work of Martin Luther King Jr.

King modeled for us the commitment to work for the liberation of both Black and white people. The Poor People's March was not merely an attempt to seek liberation for Black people but an attempt to use the civil rights movement as the context to secure economic freedom for both races. Cone's work reflects this tension.

Cone's work reflects a rugged commitment to Black power in its insistence that Black people must be set free from all the injustices that encroach upon their personhood. Yet he is equally insistent that *metanoia* must be the first step for white people in their quest for reconciliation. We must also note, however, that Black people are not let off the hook so to speak, because according to Cone, there are Black people who have lost their identity and have become white. These Blacks too must be saved. Therefore, both Black and white people must come through Blackness. In twentieth-century America, the contemporary cross is Black, and if white and Black people are to be saved, they must come through the cross of Blackness. There is no other way. Cone elucidates:

> *Contemporary Black theology, taking its cue from the black religionists of the past, believes that Christ, because he is the oppressed one whose resurrection binds him to all who are enslaved, must be inseparable from the humiliated condition of Black people. By becoming as we are in our Blackness, we now know that we are not what the world says. The knowledge of Christ frees us to be and do what we must, knowing that our Blackness has been bought with the price of his death. We are saved: saved* from *the white way of life and its dehumanizing effects on the Black community, and saved* into *the Black way of life; i.e., the freedom to be what we are and do what we must do so that Black liberation will become a reality in this land.*[10]

Although the white church and its theologians fail to accord Black people a place in its church and theology, Black theology offers white people reconciliation, but not on their own terms. White people must become Black. Gayraud Wilmore, the Black theologian, speaking for many, inquires whether or not Cone is not overly generous in allowing white people a choice to be white or Black. He inquires:

> *To say that being Black in America has little to do with skin color is, at best, only half true. It is possible to argue that in a world dominated by white power that has been inextricable from Christianity, being Black, or identifiably "Negroid," is a unique experience and has produced a unique religion, closely related to, but not exclusively bound by, the Christian tradition. Simply being oppressed or psychologically and politically in sympathy with the dispossessed does not deliver one into the experience of Blackness anymore than putting on a blindfold delivers one into the experience of being blind.*[11]

Wilmore does not share Cone's exuberance in developing an ontological perspective on Blackness that provides a window through which all people may get a vista of self. He feels that Cone needs to struggle more with the uniqueness of Blackness and its special significance for the Black community. Cone does this, but being a good theologian he has to do more than this. He relates Blackness as a category to the specificity and particularity of the Black community and at the same time shows that the symbol blackness also has ontological implications. Cone is very mindful that theology has to be both particular and universal at the same time. Theology has to be particular because it is incarnational; it is particular because it deals with people in the setting in which they live and eke out an existence for themselves. But theology also has to be universal because God, who is the subject matter of theology, is universal. So Cone uses Blackness as a category to deal with the particular situation at hand and at the same time open the door of reconciliation through which all may enter.

Cone has argued constantly that the Black church and Black theology came into being because of the failure of white religionists to relate the Gospel of Jesus to the Black community: "The appearance of Black Theology on the American scene is due exclusively to the failure of white religionists to relate the gospel of Jesus to the pain of being black in a white racist society."[12] Cone rejects the exclusionary practice of the white church/theology and insists that Black theology cannot only speak to the particularity of the Black community but also to the universality of the human situation.

There are two additional reasons that allow Cone to relate Black theology to the human situation. The first is that Cone anchors his theology in the Black church, and that church has never been exclusionary. Additionally, this openness in Cone's theology reflects the openness of the civil rights movement, in which Martin Luther King Jr. was insistent that an ethic of inclusivity was the task to which God had called the movement. King's dream included the children of former slaves and former slave masters. This was a part of the legacy that James Cone inherited.

In his second book, *A Black Theology of Liberation,* Cone offers his clearest statement on Blackness being an ontological symbol. He writes: "Blackness is an *ontological* symbol for all people who participate in the liberation of man from oppression. This is the universal note in Black theology. It believes that all people were created for freedom, and that God always sides with the oppressed against the oppressors."[13] So the universal, which seems to be lost on the horizontal level, is recaptured at a much deeper level: the psychological and the ontological. The key to Blackness has to do with one's commitment or lack of commitment to the struggle of the oppressed. It has to do with whether your body, mind, and spirit are in solidarity with the oppressed.

BLACK THEOLOGY AND THE BLACK CHURCH

We noted that one of the marks of Cone's early theology was the difficult dialogue that he joined between white church/theology and Black existence. A second mark of this early theology is its commitment to the Black church. Cone writes: "In Bearden, a small community with approximately eight hundred whites and four hundred blacks, two important realities shaped my consciousness: the black Church experience and the sociopolitical significance of white people."[14]

Cone became a member of the Macedonia A.M.E. Church at age ten and preached his first sermon in his brother's church at age sixteen. The Black church provided an alternative to the contradictions of Black life. As a child growing up in the American South in the 1950s, he came to know the grace of God as the sacred space for freedom. This space to grow was provided by the Black church. Growing up in the South, he experienced an existence in which, "White people did everything within their power to define black reality, to tell us who we were and their definition, of course, extended no further than their social, political, and economic interests. They tried to make us believe that God created Black people to be white people's servants."[15]

In this society the Black man was called "boy" and the Black woman "auntie." Black people were not respected by white people and so their dignity was compromised. It was in the Black church that this respect stolen by the white community was restored. In this church their sanctity was affirmed as sons and daughters of God. So Black people would sing:

Freedom! Oh Freedom! Oh Freedom, I love thee!
And before I'll be a slave, I'll be buried in my grave,
And go home to my Lord and be free.[16]

It is no wonder then that Cone pastored in the A.M.E. Church while a student in college. After seminary he pursued a Ph.D. degree at Northwestern University "in order to prepare myself for the teaching ministry."[17]

Cone affirms the Black church as the home of theology. Because he was immensely influenced by Karl Barth, there was no doubt in his mind that theology is accountable to the church and must serve the needs of the church. But what especially fascinated him was that he found historical precedents for the Black church to be the locus and the focus of a revolutionary theology. This was important to Cone because his passion was to relate Black power to the Black church. Affirming the revolutionary context of the Black church, he asserts that preachers such as the Reverend Highland Garnet, urged Black people to rebel against white power: "Therefore, he taught that the spirit of liberty is a gift from God, and God thus endows the slave with the zeal to break the chains of slavery."[18] Other Black church leaders such as Nat Turner, Nathaniel Paul, and Bishop McNeil Turner provided a theological baseline for Cone's explication of an ecclesiology that accommodated Black power. Cone could say: "Nat Turner, a Baptist preacher and slave, not only urged rebellion against white slave owners, but became an ardent leader of the most successful slave revolt. He felt commissioned by God to lead slaves into the new age of freedom. In 1831, he and his group killed sixty whites in twenty-four hours before they were overpowered by state and federal troops."[19]

The revolutionary ferment engendered by the pre–Civil War Black church provided a historical frame of reference for this young theologian. According to Cone, the pre–Civil War Black church influenced Martin King, allowing him to advocate breaking unjust laws. The pre–Civil War ministers of the Black church were willing to fight the system of slavery until death. The pre–Civil War Black church provided the inspiration for Martin Luther King Jr. to institute a program of civil disobedience. According to Cone, it is rather sad that in the post–Civil War period the Black church aped the white church, and it took theologians such as Martin Luther King Jr. to call the church back to themes of equality and freedom in the political and social spheres. Cone indicates his esteem for Dr. King and at the same time alludes to the debt that the Black church as a whole owes to King:

At least during the early stages this movement was a return to the spirit of the pre–Civil War black preachers with the emphasis being on freedom and equality in the present political structure. King saw clearly the meaning of the gospel with its social implications and sought to instill its true spirit in the hearts and minds of black and white in

this land. He was a man endowed with a charisma of God;
he was a prophet in our own time. And like no other black
or white American he could set black people's hearts on fire
with the gospel of freedom in Christ which would make them
willing to give up all for the cause of black humanity.[20]

King became for Cone a contemporary model of a pre–Civil War revolutionary preacher relating the gospel to the plight of Black people. Cone acknowledges, however, that King did not embrace the concept of *Black power,* yet Black power was a consequence of King's work: "Black power advocates are men who were inspired by his zeal for freedom, and Black Power is their attempt to make his dream a reality. If the Black church organizations want to remain faithful to the New Testament gospel and to the great tradition of the pre–Civil War Black church, they must relinquish their stake in the status quo and the values in white society by identifying exclusively with Black Power."[21] So King and the pre–Civil War Black church became important referents for Cone as he developed his ecclesiology.

Cone turns not only to sources within the Black church in the formulation of his theology of the church but also to white sources, especially the work of Karl Barth. Cone calls attention to the similarities that he finds between the Black religious experience and the theology of Karl Barth. Barth's articulation of a trinitarian method in the development of his theology is of special interest to Cone. Barth states that there are three primary sources for doing theology: the Word of God as preached, the Word of God as written, and the Word of God as revealed. These three sources are really one, yet they are independent; so Barth speaks of a three-ness in one-ness, and a one-ness in three-ness. Speaking of the congruencies that he finds between Barth's theology and the Black religious experience, Cone states:

When one relates Barth's theology to the black church
experience, there are many similarities. Like Barth's
theology, Jesus Christ occupies the center of the gospel

message in the black church. In sermon, song, prayer, and
testimony, Jesus is the one to whom the people turn in times
of trouble and distress, because they believe that he can heal
their wounded hearts and broken spirits. He is the one who
is called "the lily of the valley and the bright and morning
star." No black preacher would dare to "tell the story"
without reference to Jesus, because he is the gospel story.
Without him there is no story to tell and no gospel to
celebrate.[22]

The Christocentric focus of Barth's work, coupled with the confessional nature of his theology, is an important resource for Cone in the articulation of Black theology. Barth's insistence that the Bible is the primary source for theology and that the church needs to recapture its primary mission of proclaiming the Word of God all find a ready response in Cone's approach to the theological task. Cone marvels at how close the emphasis in Barth's theology approximates the reality in the Black church.

The theology in the Black church is scriptural. This dependence and reverence that the Black church has for the Bible goes back to slavery. The Bible was often the first book to which slaves were introduced. Many slaves risked floggings and death by hiding and learning to read "the good book." Further, Cone points out that Barth's insistence on the Word of God as preached resonates with the witness and the experience of the Black church. In the Black church, the high point in the worship service is the proclamation of the Word of God. In Black ecclesiology, the proclamation of the Word of God is a miracle, a miracle not of human volition but of divine revelation.

As Cone constructs his ecclesiology he uses sermons, songs, and testimonies from the Black church, but he does this in conversation with an old ally, Karl Barth: "Barth was the main nonblack influence in my writing of *Black Theology and Black Power*. My dependence was considerable; Deotis Roberts and my brother Cecil (among others) thought it excessive."[23] As Cone reveals, this dependence on Barth, Tillich, and others goes beyond his first book. I find this tendency to dialogue with white theologians and a willingness to use their work as sources emblematic of Cone's work.

Cone, however, was not uncritical of Barth's work. He complained that Barth's perception of the church was limited to the institutional church. Cone certainly went further than Barth in speaking of the church as the community of the oppressed. Here Cone is closer to King than to Barth. The wellspring from which Cone draws is King's understanding of the beloved community.

In Cone's second book, *A Black Theology of Liberation,* he not only spells out the formal sources and nature of the theological task but also gives a thorough explication of the doctrine of the church. In this book he treats the doctrine of revelation, the doctrine of God, the doctrine of Christ, and the doctrine of humanity; in one chapter, he deals with the doctrines of the church, eschatology, and the world. But all these doctrines are throughout suffused with some notion of the church as community, the church as mission, and the church as agent of social transformation.

THE CHURCH AS COMMUNITY

Theology comes to life in the church. The church is the home of theology. With Tillich and Barth, Cone calls attention to the central distinction between theology and philosophy: theology is dependent on the community for its reason for being. Theology comes to life in the church and is responsive to the needs of that community. Cone explains:

Most theologians agree that theology is a church discipline, i.e., a discipline which functions within the Christian community. This is one aspect which distinguishes theology from philosophy of religion. Philosophy of religion is not committed to the community; but it is an individual attempt to analyze the nature of ultimate reality through rational thought alone, using elements of many different religions to assist in the articulation of the ultimate. Theology by contrast cannot be separated from the community which it represents.[24]

The major problem that Cone has with the white church/theology is that its understanding of community is exclusionary. Community/ church for white church/theology means white people. Not only does this mean that the white church/theology is irrelevant to the needs of the Black community but it means that they are unchristian. Black theology transcends the exclusionary character of white church/ theology by making the community of the oppressed the normative community for church. It is this community to which Black theology is accountable and responsive. Quite often when Cone refers to the Black community he is specifically referring to the community of the oppressed. So the "God of the Oppressed" is not merely the God of Black people as a racial unit but the God of all people who are in solidarity with the oppressed. It is in this sense that the church universal is called to become Black. Cone writes:

> It is the job of the Church to become black with him
> [Christ] and accept the shame which white society places on
> blacks. But the Church knows that what is shame is holiness
> to God. Black is holy, that is, it is the symbol of God's
> presence in history on behalf of oppressed man. Where there
> is black, there is oppression; but blacks can be assured that
> where there is blackness, there is Christ who has taken on
> blackness so that what is evil in men's eyes might become
> good. Therefore Christ is black because he is oppressed, and
> oppressed because he is black. And if the Church is to join
> Christ by following his opening, it too must go where
> suffering is and become black also.[25]

Here the church is called to become like her sovereign. The church is called to become Black. In this passage Cone also highlights the dialectical use of the category blackness. On the one hand we are reminded that where there is blackness there is oppression. This is so because in the community of the oppressed, people are not nameless, faceless, and raceless, but because of their race and black faces, they are victimized and marginalized on the fringes of society.

But as we noted earlier there is also a positive meaning to the category blackness. Blackness is not only a symbol of what is wrong with the community but also a symbol of the liberating possibilities of the community. Blackness is at once a symbol of oppression and a symbol of redemption. This is why the white church/theology is called to become Black. The church has no alternative but to become Black if it is to join Christ in his work of setting people free. Christ has made the Black condition his own and the church is called to be in solidarity with him: "He meets the blacks where they are and becomes one of them. We see him there with his black face and big black hands lounging on a street corner. . . . For whites to find him with big lips and kinky hair is as offensive as it was for the Pharisees to find him partying with tax collectors. But whether whites want to hear it or not, *Christ is black, baby,* with all the features which are detestable to white society."[26]

One's relationship to this community is indicative of one's relationship to Christ. There is no such phenomenon as Christ without his people or the church without Christ. There is an indissoluble unity between Christ and his people. Therefore, the Christian church is the community that joins Christ in his struggle to set the oppressed free. The book of Matthew (25:33–40) provides a biblical point of departure for Cone's insistence that Christ is partial to the oppressed and sides with them in their struggle: "Just as you did it to one of the least of these who are members of my family, you did it to me." Jesus Christ is the essence and norm of the church's action. Black theology is Christian theology because it centers on Jesus Christ. According to Cone, there can be no Christian theology that does not have Christ as its reason for being and its point of departure. It is from the direction of Jesus Christ as the essence and norm of the church that we may expect the church's full participation in liberation.

THE CHURCH AS MISSION.

The emphasis on the church as community and Christ's involvement as its reason for being points us to Cone's view of the church as mission. The church's mission is inextricably linked to the mission of Christ. The church has no independent mission apart from Christ, so to speak of the mission of the church is at the same time to talk

about the meaning of Christ for "the oppressed Blacks of the land."
Cone explicates for us the relationship between ecclesiology and
Christology in Black theology:

> *Because Jesus Christ is the focal point for everything*
> *that is said about the Christian gospel, it is necessary to*
> *investigate the meaning of his person and work in the light*
> *of the black perspective. It is one thing to assert that he is*
> *the essence of the Christian gospel, and quite another to*
> *specify the meaning of his existence in relation to the slave*
> *ships that appeared on the American shores. Unless his*
> *existence is analyzed in the light of the oppressed of the*
> *land, we are still lost wondering what his presence means for*
> *the auction block, the Underground Railroad, and*
> *contemporary manifestations of Black Power. . . . If Christ is*
> *to have any meaning for us, he must leave the security of*
> *the suburbs by joining black people in their condition. What*
> *need have we for a white Christ when we are not white but*
> *black? If Christ is white and not black, he is an oppressor,*
> *and we must kill him.*[27]

Cone indicates that he is not interested in academic theology,
that is, a theology that is interested in probing the doctrines of
ecclesiology and Christology for the sake of investigating their logical consistency or analyzing the cogency of their classical formula-
tions: "We cannot separate our questions about Jesus from the concreteness of everyday life. We ask, who is Jesus Christ for us today?
because we believe the story of his life and death is the answer to the
human story of oppression and suffering. . . . But for Christians who
have experienced the extreme absurdities of life, the christological
question is not primarily theoretical but practical. It arises from the
encounter of Christ in the struggle for freedom."[28]

Unlike Barth and Tillich, who articulate a Christology from
above, Cone and King espouse a Christology from below. This is so
because the church as it comes to grips with its mission asks concerning Jesus: "Who is this Jesus who lightens our burdens and eases our
pain?" and the question who is Jesus? pushes back to the earlier

question, who was Jesus? To raise the question, who was Jesus?
forces us back to the gospel record, which protects the church from
making Jesus in its own image. The historical picture of Jesus contained for us in the gospel record provides checks and balances for the
church as the church ferrets out its understanding of its mission.

To understand the historical Jesus is not only to learn that Jesus
is who he was but even more important to begin to understand that
this knowledge of Jesus forces the church to see the identification of
Jesus with the poor and the marginalized. This is the main key in
which the church's understanding of its mission is to be understood.
Cone explains cogently:

> *Taking seriously the New Testament Jesus, Black
> Theology believes that the historical kernel is the
> manifestation of Jesus as the Oppressed One whose earthly
> existence was bound up with the oppressed of the land. . . .
> To understand the historical Jesus without seeing his
> identification with the poor as decisive is to misunderstand
> him and thus distort his historical person. . . . Unless the
> contemporary oppressed [church] know that the kerygmatic
> Christ is the real Christ (as Martin Kähler would put it) to
> the extent that he was completely identified with the
> oppressed of his earthly ministry, they cannot know that
> their liberation is a continuation of his work.*[29]

It is of first importance for the oppressed of the land to know
that their liberation is a continuation of the ministry of Jesus. Jesus'
past is the clue to his present activity with victims. His history
becomes the medium through which he is made accessible to us. The
key for unlocking "who is Jesus Christ for us today?" is found in the
historical kernel of the faith. The risen Messiah is the crucified
Christ. With Pannenberg, Cone asserts that if the divinity of Christ
were in conflict with his humanity, he would begin with an affirmation of the humanity of Christ as the point of departure for getting
handles on the church's mission in the world today.[30]

The focus on the historical Jesus as the point of departure for faith calls attention to the importance of Scripture as the basis of Christology and the church's self-understanding. Without this biblical-historical witness we are left with a docetic Christ, who knows nothing about the human situation.

This witness of Scripture to the historical Jesus not only calls attention to the humanity of Christ, which is essential for Black theology, but also bears witness to the social context of Christology. The sociological context of Christological inquiry opens up the possibility of understanding the importance of the claim that Jesus was a Jew. To focus on the humanity of Christ and on his Jewishness is of great importance for Black theology. The humanity of Christ calls attention to his universality, and his Jewishness points up his particularity. The emphasis on the Jewishness of Christ not only links him to the faith of Israel but also connects God's salvation drama to the Exodus-Sinai event.

The theme of the humanity of Christ has always been a central key for Black ecclesiology. The suffering and death of Christ have always been relevant themes in the life of the Black church. Hence the community of the oppressed sing:

Were you there when they crucified my Lord?
Were you there when they crucified my Lord?
Oh! sometimes it causes me to tremble, tremble,
Were you there when they crucified my Lord?

Or the Black church sings:

Dey whupped him up the hill,
dey crowned him wid a thorny crown,
dey nailed him to the cross,
dey pierced him in the side,
de blood came twinklin' down,
an' he never said a mumbalin' word,
he jes hung his head an' he died.[31]

In the Black church it is easy to connect with the biblical picture of the humanity of Christ because the biblical story teaches that he entered into solidarity with the oppressed. In the suffering of Christ, Black Christians could find a clue to the meaning of their own suffering. It is this historical basis of the faith that is crucial for an understanding of the mission of the church. The mission of the church is anchored in the biblical witness to the humanity of Christ. Jesus' past is the clue to the church's understanding of its mission in the world.

But an examination of the biblical witness to the church's norm and essence Jesus Christ shows that Jesus is not only "who he was," but that "Jesus is who he is." Black theology contends that the past does not exhaust our notions of the mission of Jesus but that the resurrection of Christ provides an interpretative key for understanding his present activity in the world. The past points to his history of solidarity and identification with victims. The resurrection points to God's way of righting the wrongs done to victims, and of the in-breaking of the liberating power of God which issues forth in the liberation of the oppressed. The crucified Christ is also the risen Savior.

It is the interplay between the church's understanding of the Jesus of history and the Christ of faith that provides the creative tension in which the church's mission is nurtured. The church does not have to choose between the Jesus of history and the Christ of faith, says Cone. The Black church has always affirmed the Jesus of history as the Christ of faith. What this means among other things, is that the Black church does not have to choose between a Christology "from below" or a Christology "from above" but rather keep both in dialectical tension, acknowledging "that Christ's meaning for us today is found in our encounter with the historical Jesus as the Crucified and Risen Lord who is present with us in the struggle for freedom."[32] As Christology informs the mission of the church, it must take with renewed seriousness both the *wasness* and the *isness* of Jesus.

The *wasness* is Christology's point of departure because it points to the inseparable unity of Christ with victims. The *isness* calls attention to the present involvement of Christ in the struggle of victims for liberation. As the church witnesses to the power of Christ's presence in their social existence they are led to ask; "What manner of man is this?" Someone may reply:

> *He is my helper in time of distress,*
> *He is the one that's been good to me,*
> *He gave me victory, the Son of the Almighty God we serve.*

Or another in the church may testify:

> *He is the one who makes things right,*
> *and that's why I have to "steal away" to him in prayer,*
> *for "I ain't got long to stay here."*
> *He is the one who "calls me by the thunder,"*
> *and "he calls me by the lightning,"*
> *"the trumpet sounds within my soul";*
> *and then I know that I ain't got long to stay here.*[33]

Black people were able to survive the atrocities of slavery and the lynchings and brutalities meted out by the slave master and a vicious system of slavery because of the confidence that Christ was not merely a historical figure of first-century Palestine but that he was alive and "would make a way out of no way."

With the mission of the crucified and risen Christ as its clue, the church cannot allow itself to become passive and nonfeeling in relation to pain and suffering but like Christ must be willing to become a revolutionary community, breaking laws that destroy persons and refusing to be at ease in Zion. When the mission of the Christ becomes the mission of the church, the church will insist on participating in the liberating struggles of the world. The church will become involved in the world. It cannot be otherwise, because this is where the church will find Christ. Cone articulates succinctly the mission of the church:

To preach the gospel today means confronting the world with the reality of human freedom. It means telling black people that their slavery has come to an end, and telling whites to let go of the chains. Black people do not have to live according to white rules. If the gospel is "the power of God unto salvation," then black people have a higher loyalty to him that cuts across every sphere of human existence. Preaching the gospel is nothing but proclaiming to blacks that they do not have to submit to ghetto-existence. Our new existence has been bought and paid for; we are now redeemed, set free. Now it is incumbent upon us to behave as free persons.[34]

Cone in an incisive and insightful way calls attention to the way in which Christology is normative for the church's understanding of faith and action. The gospel is one of freedom, and because of the death and resurrection of Christ, the loyalty of oppressed people is first and foremost to him, and not to the gods of culture. Black people should refuse to submit to ghetto-like conditions because their freedom has been bought and paid for. Therefore Black people should obey the gospel and live as children of freedom.

There are two emphases in Cone's view of the mission of the church we should consider. First, there are themes in his understanding of the mission of the church which are rather traditional: that is, the church is called to proclaim Jesus Christ "the power of God unto salvation." Further, the church must proclaim that the oppressed have been set free, and "sin has no more dominion over them." The oppressed therefore must live as free people and not as slaves. This gospel of liberation is the content of the church's preaching and must remain so because it was the essence of the life and ministry of Jesus: "The gospel is the proclamation of God's liberation as revealed in the event of Jesus and the outpouring of the Holy Spirit."[35]

The second emphasis is that this preaching and sharing of the gospel has a nontraditional focus, because it proclaims the gospel in situations where the socioeconomic and political structures are aligned against people and God. It is one thing to announce that individuals can be converted; it is quite another to believe that institutions and structures can be converted. Cone insists that true preaching must address the principalities and powers such as racism, sexism, poverty, classism, and social and economic exploitation.

The church is that community that lives on the basis of the radical demands of the gospel by making the gospel a social, economic, and political reality. The church has to risk living out the gospel in a society that refuses to believe the gospel. It risks going against the grain of the society because the church dares to be like her Savior.

This attempt to relate the gospel to the plight of the poor in such a way that the social context in which they live comes in for sociopolitical analysis echoes the life and ministry of Martin Luther King Jr. Speaking to fellow clergy persons at the Riverside Church in New York City, Martin King reminds them that his calling as a minister disallows him the privilege of remaining silent when he ponders the destruction of life and property in Vietnam:

> *Since I am a preacher by trade, I suppose it is not surprising that I have several reasons for bringing Vietnam into the field of my moral vision. . . . Perhaps the more tragic recognition of reality took place when it became clear to me that the war was doing far more than devastating the hopes of the poor at home. It was sending their sons and their brothers and their husbands to fight and to die in extraordinary high proportions relative to the rest of the population. We were taking the black young men who had been crippled by our society and sending them 8,000 miles away to guarantee liberties in Southeast Asia which they had not found in Southwest Georgia and East Harlem. So we have been repeatedly faced with the cruel irony of watching Negro and white boys on TV screens as they kill and die together for a nation that has been unable to seat*

them together in the same schools. . . . I could not be silent
in the face of such cruel manipulation of the poor.[36]

Further, King points out that many people counseled him to
steer clear of peace issues. After all, he was only a civil rights
activist and he should limit his ministry to agitation within that
purview. He reminds his audience that when the Southern Leadership Conference was formed in 1957 its motto was: "To save the
soul of America." There were no off-limit signs indicating parame-
ters within which the gospel should be related. The gospel as it was
embodied in the mission of the church should be addressed to the
whole world.

THE CHURCH AS AGENT OF SOCIAL TRANSFORMATION

We noted that Cone speaks of the church as the community of
the oppressed and that the church's mission cannot be separated
from the mission of Christ. Now we must note the third focus, the
church as agent of transformation.

According to Black theology, transformation is constitutive of
the nature of the church. Transformation is not extrinsic to the nature
of the church but is intrinsic to it. It is in this context that Cone
fleshes out his perception of the eschatological grounding of hope as
the basis for the politics of liberation. Political praxis becomes the
main key for the church's engagement of the world. Because of this,
the church cannot any longer talk about Christian hope without
meaningfully relating it to the struggle of oppressed people in history for liberation.

Hope for Cone is more than the anticipation of liberation. It is
both the motive force and the shape of human liberation. The vision
of the eschatological reign of God makes Christians dissatisfied with
reality as they know it and provides the courage for them to turn the
world up-side-down. To be in the realm of God means to live with
two warrants at once. On the one hand, it means accepting God's
grace and being willing to give up everything for it. This is what

repentance means. On the other hand, to be in the realm of of God means to fight for the creation of a new world. This is necessary because the Christ who is at work in the Black church is not the "Christ of culture" but the "Christ who transforms culture." Cone writes: "The event of the kingdom today is the liberation struggle in the black community. It is where people are suffering and dying for want of human dignity. It is thus incumbent upon all to see the event for what it is—God's kingdom. This is what conversion means. Black people are being converted because they see in the events around them the coming of the Lord, and will not be scared into closing their eyes to it."[37]

The new future that the coming reign of God announces begins with a transformation of the present conditions that hold people hostage. Hope then must become historical activity and issue forth in concrete acts of liberation in the here and now. It is in this sense that heaven on the lips of Black people pointed toward a radical eschatological vision in which the community of the oppressed share the hope and possibility of bringing into existence a new social order in which values such as justice, love, forgiveness, kindness, and integrity can find full expression.

Cone points out that heaven had a double meaning on the lips of Black people. On the one hand, heaven referred to the realization of this worldly goals such as freedom to the North or the manifestation of liberation in the here and now. This is illustrated in the case of Frederick Douglass' view of the promised land on the "other side of Jordan." For Harriet Tubman, heaven meant reaching the North. Tubman could say after reaching free territory during slavery: "I looked at my hands to see if I was the same person now that I was free. Dere was such a glory over everything, the sun came like gold thru the trees, and over the fields, and I felt like I was in heaven." Tubman was not content to be free while others remained in bondage. She returned to the South nine times taking others with her to the North where they could be free.

Cone insists that eschatology must become social and political action aimed at the creation of a new society. In the light of the coming reign of God, not only does the oppressed community see in the past structures that need to be overthrown, structures that humiliate and seek to enslave the oppressed, but through the inbreaking of the new vision, the community sees the transforming hand of God pointing the way to a new reality. It is the hand of the transcendent God shaping a new future. Drawing on an eschatology latent in the Black community, James Cone states:

> By contrast, black people's talk about hope, though contemporary with Marx, did not arise out of the dialogue with Marxism. Black religion and its emphasis on hope came into being through black people's encounter with the Crucified and risen Lord in the context of American slavery. In their encounter with Jesus Christ, black slaves received "a vision from on high" wherein they were given a new knowledge of their personhood, which enabled them to fight for the creation of a world by black affirmations. Their hope sprang from the actual presence of Jesus, breaking into their broken existence, and bestowing upon them a foretaste of God's promised freedom. They could fight against slavery and not give up in despair, because they believed that their earthly struggle was a preparation for the time when they would "cross over Jordan" "and walk in Jerusalem just like John."[38]

This unwillingness to put asunder what God has joined together —the eschatological and the concrete historical—which characterizes the Black spiritual ethos, is what has uniquely equipped the Black church in its long march toward freedom and human liberation in this country. The Black church became not only the symbol of the coming future reign of God but the agent of social transformation for Black people. According to Cone, it was the encounter of Black Christians with the crucified and risen Savior that provided the inspirational source and the sustaining power for the community of the oppressed as they sought change in the social, economic, and political foundations of society. Cone writes: "Christ's salvation is liberation; there is no liberation without Christ. Both meanings are inherent in the statement that Jesus Christ is the ground of human liberation. Any statement that divorces salvation from liberation or makes human freedom independent of divine freedom must be rejected."[39]

Cone is quite correct in insisting that human freedom is to be grounded in divine freedom if the church as moral agent of transformation is to take on the principalities and powers that hold God's children in captivity. For the people to maintain their confidence in the struggle for freedom and "to keep on keeping on" even when they are tired and the signs of victory are not visible is to presuppose the divine presence. It is to have faith in the ultimate victory of God's love over everything that contradicts and opposes it. Black theology asserts that God in Jesus Christ entered human history and engaged the forces of oppression in combat and has decisively defeated them. Divine freedom has broken the power of human bondage. Cone writes: "The Bible, it is important to note, does not consist of units of infallible truth about God or Jesus. Rather, it tells the story of God's will to redeem humankind from sin, death, and Satan. According to the New Testament witnesses, God's decisive act against these powers happened in Jesus' life, death and resurrection."[40] And: "Though the decisive battle against evil has been fought and won, the war, however, is not over."[41] It is because the battle has been won that the church as the agent of liberation witnesses change that is already taking place in the present. The church is called to live as if there is no permanence to the present order of injustice. The church through its ministry of transformation claims that this evil age is on its way out and the new age of God's righteousness is on its way in. What God has effected historically in the life, death, and resurrection of Jesus Christ, God accomplishes daily through the self-determination of the community of the oppressed. The presence of the crucified and risen Savior in the community of the oppressed empowers this community to say yes to all that affirms its right to liberation and no to all that encroaches on and frustrates its being. Liberation then becomes shouting no to exploitation and victimization of all sorts and acknowledging that these evils do not have their foundation in God's will.

Cone raises the issue as to whether or not the call for transformation in the society is at the same time a call for socioeconomic analysis that takes the structures of oppression seriously. "Does faith need something more?" he asks. Does the gospel have within it the tools to help oppressed people analyze evils such as racism, capitalism, classism, poverty, sexism, and ageism? Cone concludes that faith needs something more and asks us to consider the possibility that a part of the more that faith needs is Marxism.

Marxism should not be cursorily dismissed without consideration because it helps Black theology to focus on and to question the social context of reality. Further, Marxism helps oppressed people understand that white theology tells them more about the theologians and their culture than it tells them about God. It helps the oppressed understand that theology is interested speech. In the case of white theology, it reflects the dominant culture. Hence the ruling ideas reflect the material relationships of the dominant culture. This observation is a break through for Black people, claims Cone, because it forces Black theology to consider the role of economics and politics in the definition of truth.

Sociology then becomes the midwife of theology. Theology is able, with the help of sociology, to analyze who owns the means of production and to what extent the poverty of the poor is contrived. Further, Black theology begins to discover that the social arrangements of society reflect the interests of the dominant class and race. And one reason why the ruling class helps to promote religion is because it serves as a sedative for the oppressed, preventing them from questioning the social and material arrangements of society. Religion often makes the oppressed comfortable in their misery and poverty. Cone writes:

> *The importance of Marx for our purposes is his insistence that thought has no independence from social existence. In view of his convincing assertion that*

*"consciousness can never be anything else than conscious
existence," theologians must ask, "what is the connection
between dominant material relations and the ruling ideas in
a given society?" And even if they do not accept the rigid
causality of so-called orthodox Marxists, theologians will
find it hard to avoid the truth that their thinking about
things divine is closely intertwined with the "manifestations
of actual life." A serious encounter with Marx will make
theologians confess their limitations, their inability to say
anything about God that is not at the same time a statement
about the social context of their existence.*[42]

So then in an attempt to answer the important question, does
faith need something more? Cone suggests that faith needs a social
theory to help faith analyze the structures of oppression and thereby
expose systemic evil. Although it is clear that Cone finds the Marxist analysis of capitalism and social consciousness helpful, he is not
uncritical of Marxist thought nor does he believe it is adequate as a
critical tool for Black theology. He points to the limits of Marxism
for Black theology: " I reject dogmatic Marxism that reduces every
contradiction to class analysis and thus ignores racism as a legitimate point of departure in the process of liberation. There are racist
Marxists as there are racist capitalists, and we must struggle against
both."[43]

Black theology does not find it necessary to exclude Marxist
analysis but coupled with that must be the work of scholars such as
W. E. B. DuBois, Malcolm X, Daniel Payne, David Walker, and
Martin Luther King Jr. Cone credits King for pointing the Black
church in the right direction by joining social transformation and
eschatology. King gave the church a vision of what it was called to
become and insisted that transformation should not take place outside the church only, but also within. Perhaps it was because Cone
was speaking in Atlanta, the birthplace and home of Martin King,
that he credits theology to the vision of Martin Luther King. He
states: "Without this dream of freedom, so vividly expressed in the

life, teachings, and death of Jesus, Malcolm and Martin, there would be no Black theology." Cone adds: "If people have no dreams they will accept the world as it is and will not seek to change it. To dream is to know that what "is ain't suppose to be." No one in our time expressed this eschatological note more clearly than Martin Luther King, Jr."[44]

But to dream is not enough. Eschatology must be coupled with social analysis. This was one of the lasting contributions that Martin King made to Black theology: his insistence that unless dreams were socially analyzed they would vanish into the night. Cone writes:

This is one of the important principles we learned from Martin King and many black preachers who worked with him. Real substantial change in societal structures requires scientific analysis. King's commitment to social analysis not only characterized his involvement in the Civil Rights Movement but also led him to take a radical stand against the war in Vietnam. It is to his credit that he never allowed a pietistic faith in the other world to become a substitute for good judgment in this world. He not only preached sermons about the Promised Land but concretized his vision with a political attempt to actualize his hope.[45]

As the Black church seeks to actualize its dreams, it must note that to dream is not enough. Faith needs more than eschatology: indeed, faith must insist that eschatology becomes history. As Black theology seeks to translate dreams into reality, it must be willing to listen to Jesus, Malcolm, Martin, and last but not least, Marx.

In the final chapter of his book *For My People,* Cone gives an exposition of what it would look like for the church to become involved in social transformation. He begins the chapter with a quotation from Martin King and an earlier one from Malcolm X, which provide useful clues to the church's involvement in social change. In the citation from King, the church is challenged to engage in the restructuring of American society. King points out that it is unacceptable that America, the richest country on earth, would have forty million poor people. To raise the question as to why this should happen is to begin to ask about the redistribution of our resources: "And when you begin to ask that question, you are raising questions about the economic system, about a broader distribution of wealth. When you ask that question, you begin to question the capitalistic economy. And I'm simply saying that more and more, we've got to begin to ask questions about the whole society. . . . But one day we must come to see that an edifice which produces beggars needs restructuring."[46]

Cone is insistent that the Black church needs to create a vision of a new social order that deals with the complexities of the world in which they live. The challenge facing the church is to build on the vision of our past leaders. Malcolm's vision of nationalism and Martin's vision of the beloved community are inadequate tools for analysis as the Black community faces the twenty-first century. The methods and ideals of the past are incapable of dealing effectively with the challenges of the present and the future. The church's commitment to the transformation of the world requires a new vision. The new vision of freedom must build on the dream of our leaders of the past but it must move beyond North America to include the third world. This new vision must be able to analyze world poverty and sickness, monopoly capitalism, antidemocratic socialism, racism, and sexism with a determination to eliminate these evils.

Black theology acknowledges that the Black community has made substantial gains through the electoral process. Through the ballot, Black mayors have been elected in Atlanta, Los Angeles, Chicago, and Detroit to name a few cities. The community has even helped the Reverend Jesse Jackson mount a serious bid for the presidency of the United States of America. But these gains have not altered the situation of poverty for the masses. Although political action is a step towards freedom in that it forces Black people to take responsibility for their future, Cone is quite clear that political action is not the answer: "The goal of black freedom must mean more than a share or parity in the current American capitalist system. That would mean only a few jobs and privileges for black professionals and continued misery for the masses of Blacks in the U.S.A."[47] The placing of mayors in major cities does not make any lasting difference for the Black masses because the capitalist system that advocates the maximization of profit is still intact. Profit is the main key in which these systems are set and it really does not matter whether the chief administrator is white or Black. The poor masses get screwed every time.

At the national level, about 1 percent of the population controls over 30 percent of the wealth. In the third world, the situation is even bleaker: the United States and Western Europe, which compose about 17 percent of the world's population, control more than 70 percent of the world's wealth. Each day more than fifty thousand people die of hunger and malnutrition. These are mainly people of color.

The recital of these facts means that the Black church can no longer sit back and allow others to run the world. This is the same world for which Jesus died. To be a Christian is to love thy neighbor and this includes making the world a more human place for that neighbor. The Black church has no alternative but to become the agent of transformation in the world Jesus died to redeem. The death and resurrection place a special burden and responsibility on Black churches. Cone challenges the church:

Are we going to continue to preach the same old sermons, pray the same old prayers, and sing the same old songs as if that alone would be enough for the establishment of freedom in the twenty-first century? Are we going to continue with the same old church meetings and conferences—electing officers and bishops, holding revivals and hearing charismatic speakers, buying old white churches and constructing new ones, appointing and calling pastors on the basis of a superficial emotional appeal, shouting and testifying for the saints, while the world around us continues toward destruction? Is that all we have to offer Black people?[48]

The two central ingredients for the church's involvement in transformation arc faith and analysis. The church must begin to radically question the way society is organized. Faith is not enough. The "more" that faith needs is analysis. But the very nature of the church makes it impossible for the church to accentuate analysis and minimize faith. It is within the circle of faith that the Christian finds resources for the struggle and the ability to transcend self and environment. Faith coupled with analysis issues forth in transformative justice. A faith that does not express itself in the criticism of unjust structures becomes at best the opium of the oppressed.

The temptation confronting the Black church is for it to retreat to preaching as usual, praying and business as usual, as it avoids the demands of justice in the world of racism, sexism, materialism, and classism. Authentic liberation demands a questioning of the structures of injustice that deny God's children the possibility to be fully human. But this transformation for which Black theology pleads must also express itself within the church in a transformation of values. According to Black theology, there is a danger that the Black church is aping the dominant culture and so there is an urgent need for prophetic self-criticism within the church. Cone pleads for a new social vision that will spell transformation both within and without the church.

This vision will include an emphasis on Black unity and at the same time incorporate the best of the integrationist tradition as Martin Luther King Jr. articulated it. King's vision of the "beloved community" would provide the basis for talk about this unity in community, which is the essential ingredient of this new order.

The Marxist critique of monopoly capitalism is a necessity of this new socialist democratic order that Cone posits. Basic human rights such as the right to shelter, food, work, and play must be secured for all people. The vision must be global, involving all third world people in a "rainbow coalition." This vision must be rooted in the grace of God and in the hopes and prereflective visions of the poor.

We have noted two themes that constantly emerge in the theology of James Cone: (a) The difficult dialogue between Black theology and white theology/church; and (b) The mission of the church as community of the oppressed, the mission of the church as the mission of Christ in the world, and the church as agent of transformation. Now we must look at a third theme, which runs like a black thread throughout his work: namely, theology and ethics.

THEOLOGY AND ETHICS

As early as 1970, James Cone wrote an article titled "Black Power, Black Theology, and the Study of Theology and Ethics." The central issue in this article is the relationship between Black consciousness and the Gospel of Jesus Christ. The problem for the Black church, as Cone sees it, is that many Christians posit a discontinuity between the Black experience and Jesus Christ, having internalized the teaching of the white church. This is so because most white theologians and ethicists contend that Christianity is color blind, having no particular interest in color. These theologians and ethicists claim that for Christianity to focus on color is to deny the universal note that is the very essence of Christianity. This line of reasoning, says Cone, is antithetical to Black theology and Black power because it denies blackness, which is the very essence of Black humanity.[49]

Black theology affirms blackness as the Black community's way of being in a hostile world that seeks to strip Black people of their sanctity and dignity. When white theologians and ethicists seek a meaningful way to deal with the Black/white confrontation, they advocate an ethic of love as the best way to create a situation of reconciliation. But this is potentially dangerous, claims Cone, because in essence this approach to love and reconciliation does not yet come to grips with the complexity of liberation in the Black community. A great deal of talk about reconciliation excludes any meaningful analysis of liberation as a necessary stage on the way to reconciliation. Therefore Black people need to be careful of white injunctions to love the oppressor because this call for love and reconciliation are subtle attempts of the white community to emasculate Black people. Black theology and Black ethics must reject the advice of white people when they admonish the Black community to turn the other cheek. The community must make its own decisions concerning what is necessary for the realization of its full humanity. Cone sides with Malcolm X: "We say with Brother Malcolm: 'Its not possible to love a man whose chief purpose in life is to humiliate you and still be considered a normal human being.' "[50]

Theology and ethics must function within the dialectical tension of blackness and whiteness, being and nonbeing. And as it chooses being, or blackness, as its point of departure for talk about God, humanity, and the world, it must live with the observation of the radicals that the oppressed cannot free themselves with the faith of the oppressor. We cannot free ourselves with other people's stories. We can only free ourselves with our own stories. So the Black community must adopt a hermeneutics of suspicion toward regard to any faith that is imposed on it, especially when the intent of the faith is to make Black people docile and subservient. For the Black church to believe what the oppressors say about God, humanity, and Christ is tantamount to believing the evening news report.

What the radicals are advocating is not the rejection of Christianity but the rejection of its distortions. The radicals insist that we return to the essence of the faith. If this is the case, then advocacy would be consistent with the demands of the gospel itself that we be faithful to the message of Jesus Christ. The radicals force us to ask: what relevance does Jesus Christ have for the Black community? It goes without saying that neither white theologians or ethicists have made this question central to their approach to theology or ethics. Cone concludes that they need to be liberated from the bondage of racism:

> *Theology and ethics need to undergo a revolutionary transformation so that the meaning of Christ and his church can be defined in the light of the weak and the helpless rather than according to the economic and political interests of the oppressors. My purpose is to investigate what is*

involved in such a transformation, placing special emphasis on American theology and ethics in relation to Black power and Black theology.[51]

According to Cone, when one presses white theologians on the lack of a Black perspective in their theology, they claim that the issues raised concerning Black oppression and racism properly belong to the realm of ethics. Here, Cone reminds us that ethics is from the Greek word *ethos,* meaning "custom" and "character." Cone points out that "'custom' refers to that which holds human society together. It is . . . the 'cement' of human society, providing stability and security indispensable to the living of human life."[52] At the same time ethicists usually refer to ethics as "reflections upon the foundations and principles of behavior," they speak of morality, which is derived from the latin *mos,* as "behavior according to custom." What is of special interest is that for American ethicists, the investigation of the foundation and principles of behavior always seems to coincide with the ethos of the society as defined by white people. Right behavior always seems to mean white behavior, that which is in the best interest of white people. By and large both white theologians and white ethicists have neglected the liberation of the oppressed as a major concern. Here and there one finds ethical niceties admonishing whites to be nice to Blacks.

This marked absence of Black people and their work in white theology and ethics is paralleled by the same absence in other disciplines, such as history, sociology, psychology, and other areas of life and thought in America. One of the definitions of *black* in *Merriam Webster's Collegiate Dictionary* is "thoroughly evil" or "wicked." This white view of blackness has social, political, and economic implications for Black people. Socially this means that Black people are unacceptable: they are the outcast. Black people are "Them and They." To be "Them and They" is to be separated from "We and Us." The fundamental reality in America regarding race relations is that the two races are a separated brethren. This is true of the American church and society.

The political implication of agreeing with this white view of Blackness is to further see Black people as fit for enslavement, disenfranchisement, and segregation from centers of power without any meaningful opportunity for due process of law. The police often behave as if Black people have no rights that white people have to respect. The economic implications of this view is that it is alright for Black people to be unemployed, to starve, and to be consigned to ghettos and prisons. The theological implication of this view is that God is "abstract love" with no interest in color.

Black theology emerged in rebuttal and in defiance of this Euro-American view of Blackness. Black theology asserts that in a world in which Black people are victimized and humiliated because of the color of their skin, theology and ethics are required to ask for the meaning of Jesus Christ in a situation of Black suffering and humiliation. Christian ethics and theology cannot be separable from the humiliated condition of the exploited.

Black theology and Black power contend that Blackness is the primary datum of the Black experience that must be analyzed because it is the *reason* for our oppression and the *tool* for our liberation. Speaking of Black power in relation to Black theology, Cone states:

> Black power investigates the meaning of Blackness from the political, economic, and social condition of Black people, explicating what freedom and self-determination mean for the wretched of the earth. Black theology places the Black power concept in its proper theological context, analyzing Black liberation in the light of the gospel of Jesus Christ. Black theology is the theological arm of Black power, and Black power is the political arm of Black theology.[53]

Black power analyzes the structures that exploit Black people. And in North America, the central theological problem is racism. Black power helps the victims of racism to see that from top to bottom America is racist and that the victims have two responses: accommodation or rebellion. These alternatives are really a choice between death on the one hand and life on the other, because accommodation is suicide. To accommodate is to commit political or philosophical suicide. Accommodation is the loss of community or identity. It allows white people to decide what is best for Black people and causes the community to lose its soul.

Black power rejects accommodation as a responsible response to racism. Black power provides the "courage to be" in the midst of nonbeing. From a political and sociological point of view, it does not seem possible that Black people, who are outnumbered by whites and who do not have the police force on their side, can somehow define the limits of their own existence. This ability to define their existence becomes a distinct possibility for the oppressed when they know who they are and are willing to die to protect the sanctity of their identity. Cone writes:

> This means that self-knowledge and power are two sides of the same reality. If a person knows who he is but is unable to protect his identity, there is always the possibility that he will deny that knowledge in order to affirm or identify with that which is consistent with the ruler's view of humanity. In that way, he avoids conflicts and perhaps stays alive. Such a person does not really know self. Truly to know self is to be prepared to die protecting what one knows.[54]

It is precisely at this point that Christology becomes crucial for the Black community, because Black theology claims that in the life, death, and resurrection of Jesus of Nazareth there is an unprecedented disclosure of who we are as a people and who we are called to become. It is from the perspective of Jesus Christ that the community defines itself. The humanity of our community resides in Jesus Christ. It is from the vantage point of our solidarity with him that we claim our humanity. Black theology asserts two Christological moments as critical for its-self understanding. The first is the history of Jesus in which he identified with the wretched of the earth, in the end dying between two thieves on a hill far away. Jesus' act of taking human oppression upon himself was not an historical accident but a choice that witnesses to his identification with victims today.

The second Christological moment that Black theology asserts is that through the cross and resurrection, Christ offers victims possibilities of liberation from their present situation. Cone explains: "To encounter him, the resurrected and exalted Christ who now is present as the Holy Spirit, is to encounter the possibilities and certainties of human existence which transcend the value structures of oppressive societies."[55] It is this Christ who empowers the community to rebel against all that would deny it its God-given dignity This Christ became the "last," teaching us that in God's eyes the "last" is "first." It is this new knowledge which that allows the oppressed to rebel against all that encroaches on their right to freedom.

Because Christ takes our condition upon himself, we know that we are not what the world says we are. Because of Christ's death and resurrection we are saved from the white way of life and its dehumanizing effects upon us, saved into the Black way of life. The resurrection of Christ binds him to our humiliated condition and his presence in our community opens up for us liberation vistas of the humanity to which God has called us.

As Christian ethics investigates the meaning of "stability and security," Black Christians must acknowledge that these terms cannot mean "law and order." The Black church must acknowledge that stability and security are found in Jesus Christ as the community joins him in the liberation of humanity: "He and he alone is the only norm for ethical principles and behavior; and he is found only among the poor and weak, sharing in their condition and revealing to them what must be done for their liberation."[56]

This means that Black theology avoids abstract principles dealing with right and wrong. There is only one principle: "An unqualified commitment to the oppressed Black community as that community seeks to define its existence in accordance with God's liberating activity in the world."[57] It is from within the community that guidelines for our life together must emerge.

THEOLOGICAL FOUNDATIONS FOR CHRISTIAN ETHICS

In his important work *God of the Oppressed,* Cone explores the theological foundations for Christian ethics. He is insistent that the ethical question "What am I to do?" cannot be separated from the theological question "What has God done?" The joining of these two questions not only calls attention to the inextricable connection between theology and ethics but further indicates that theology is the foundation of Christian ethics. This should not surprise us because Christian theology, like Christian ethics, occurs within the church and is accountable to the church. Cone describes the relationship of ethics and theology:

> *Thus Christian theology is the foundation of Christian ethics. Theology is the Church's reflection upon the meaning of its faith claim that God's revelation is identical with the historical freedom of the weak and the helpless. Ethics derived from theology is that branch of the Church's reflection that investigates the implication of faith in divine liberation for Christian life in the World. Formally, Christian theology asks, "Who is God?" and ethics asks, "What must we do?"*[58]

Black theology points out that the attempt to relate theology and ethics is not original to Black theology or to current theologies of liberation. Most theologians make the connection between divine revelation and ethical obedience and thereby assert the indissoluble connection between theology and ethics.

The problem with this approach in the past is twofold. On the one hand, these theologians have grounded their ethic in the status quo rather than in some notion of the freedom of God as this is expressed in the divine election of the oppressed. On the other hand, because they neglect the oppressed community in their eagerness to assert the universal character of theological discourse, these theologians also effect a divorce between theology and its biblical source. Cone writes: "Instead of standing unquestionably with the outcasts and downtrodden, as the God of the Bible does, their ethic did more to preserve the status quo than to change it. Whatever else the gospel might be, it can never be identified with the established power of the state."[59]

Theologians such as Augustine and Thomas Aquinas were guilty of identifying the will of the status quo with the will of God. This is especially true of the way they viewed slavery. Whenever our understanding of God is not derived from the biblical understanding of liberation, Christian ethics will be indifferent to the struggle of the oppressed.

The Scriptures are for the community and not for the exclusive use of experts. Hence Black people cannot trust the white experts to interpret the Scriptures for them. People in power always interpret the Scriptures according to their own interests. The Black community must remember that we cannot free ourselves with other people's stories. We must put our story in dialogue with the biblical story. It is in the conversation between the biblical story and the Black experience that we find an answer to the ethical question, "What am I to do."

Cone agrees with Paul Lehmann in *Ethics in a Christian Context* that Christian ethics has to do with knowing God's will and doing God's will. Further, Cone agrees with Lehmann that the context is the point of departure for Christian ethics, since it is within the *koinonia* that God's will becomes intelligible. Cone points out, however, that Lehmann makes the same mistake that Luther, Calvin, and John Wesley made in their attempt to talk about divine revelation in general and universal terms rather than to focus with specificity on the words and deeds of victims in the community of the oppressed: "We cannot know or hear the will of God apart from the social context of the oppressed community where Jesus is found calling us into being for freedom."[60]

This is why covenant-obedience in the community of the oppressed is not based on an ought but rather on the divine/human encounter. It is this encounter with the divine presence that defines and determines the Christian's behavior. To live as a Christian is to be what God has made us: liberated for the freedom of humanity. This means that ethics becomes an act of faith because the oppressed refuse to give their allegiance and loyalty to ethical and moral propositions as a guide for conduct but rather act from within a faith perspective hammered out in the community of the oppressed. This is so because God's will is not a code of principles or information or propositions but a relationship that the community has with Christ. Cone writes: "For Christians, Jesus is the source for what we do; without his power to make life human, our behavior would count as nothing. For Jesus is the criterion of our ethical conduct."[61] What is being advocated is not that an image of the first-century Christ serve as a model (and exemplar) for Black Christians but rather that the Black church discovers what Christ is up to in the world today and in conversation with Scripture, tradition, and the testimony of other victims allows their actions to become the risk of faith. There is no certainty that faith will not let them down sometimes. The only certainty is that Christ has promised never to leave us.

This grounding of faith and ethics in the community of the oppressed not only saves ethics from being merely a theoretical task but presses it to become a practical task with its possibilities and limits being decided from time to time in the Black community. According to Cone: "A black Christian ethic cannot ignore the fact that we are an African people, and that heritage must be recognized in ethical analysis if we are going to suggest moral directions to black people that do not violate the very substance of our being."[62]

The Black community is challenged to take its history seriously combined with an openness toward other victims irrespective of their religious persuasion. Cone cites Malcolm X:

> *What you and I need to do is to forget our differences. When we come together, we don't come together as Baptists or Methodists. You don't catch hell because you're a Baptist, and you don't catch hell because you're a Methodist or*

Baptist, you don't catch hell because you're a Democrat or a Republican, you don't catch hell because you're a Mason or an Elk, and you sure don't catch hell because you're an American; because if you were an American, you wouldn't catch hell. You catch hell because you're a black man. You catch hell, all of us catch hell for the same reason.[63]

This sense of our common humanity as a people provides an openness for participation in each other's struggle. This openness allows us to turn to each other rather than on each other.

VIOLENCE AND NONVIOLENCE: A MISPLACED DEBATE

There are few issues on which Cone is as clear as his discussion of violence. He liberates the discussion from a theoretical analysis of the pros and cons of violence versus nonviolence without any due regard for victims. Cone states the problem for us:

I contend, therefore, that the problem of violence is not the problem of a few black revolutionaries but the problem of a whole social structure which outwardly appears to be ordered and respectable but inwardly is "ridden by psychopathic obsessions and delusions"—racism and hatred. Violence is embedded in American law, and it is blessed by the keepers of moral sanctity.[64]

Cone insists that violence is a part of the fabric of the American way of life. To debate the issue of violence and nonviolence is to misplace the problem. The critical issue concerns *whose* violence.

The attempt by oppressors to contrast force and violence is specious argues Cone. Christian theologians and ethicists often argue that force is given to the state by God and is used by the state to preserve order whereas violence is force used by victims against the state. Black theology claims that this distinction is not only false but seeks to identify with the state against victims. The temptation here is for victims to accept the values of the oppressor. Even to broach the question, Are you nonviolent? is already to buy into the structure of values represented by the oppressor. As the issue of violence is broached, people tend to take sides. We are forced to side either with the oppressed or the oppressor and to signify in whose violence we participate. Cone indicates that the oppressed in their determination to create a new humanity must be willing to liberate all victims.

It is precisely at this point that Cone calls attention to the central difference between his refusal to couch the issues in terms of violence and nonviolence and Martin Luther King Jr.'s insistence that these are the issues and that nonviolence is an appropriate method to change the structural injustice in society. Cone contends that King's willingness to allow the view of love found in liberal theology to inform his social analysis makes his analysis of violence in America faulty.

Violence for Martin King was an impractical and immoral way for victims to secure justice in this society. Violence was immoral because destructive means cannot secure constructive ends. Violence was impractical philosophically because the universe is on the side of love and justice. Hence violence and counterviolence will ultimately destroy both the oppressed and the oppressor. So the real issue for King was not violence and nonviolence but nonviolence or nonexistence, community or chaos.

King anticipates Cone in his address to the clergy and laity at the Riverside Church a year before he was gunned down:

I am convinced that if we are to get on the right side of the world revolution, we as a nation must undergo a radical revolution of values. We must rapidly begin to shift from a "thing oriented" society to a "person oriented" society. When machines and computers, profit motives and property rights are considered more important than people, the giant triplets of racism, materialism, and militarism are incapable of being conquered. . . . True compassion is more than flinging a coin to a beggar; it is not haphazard and superficial. It comes to see that an edifice which produces beggars needs restructuring.[65]

CONE AND KING

There are many points at which Cone's work correlates with that of Martin Luther King Jr., his teacher and mentor. Both worked for the creation of a new humanity. And although an initial reading of Cone's work may indicate his dissatisfaction and displeasure with the church being at ease in Zion, even that dissatisfaction is aimed at pressing the church, white and Black, to be more than they are. Although this holy displeasure also appears in King's work, it is not as readily apparent as in Cone's, perhaps because at the heart of Cone's work is a difficult dialogue between Black theology and the white church/theology. At the heart of this dialogue, however, is the call for liberation, which will eventually lead to reconciliation: reconciliation is an eschatological possibility for Cone.

The dialogue with Martin King was most helpful for Cone as he hammered out an understanding of liberation in quest of reconciliation. This quest for liberation and reconciliation forced Cone to articulate an understanding of Blackness that was inclusive of both the Black and white communities. Granted that for Cone, unlike Martin King, reconciliation is a minor key that must be understood within the more strident notes of liberation, it is nonetheless understood as a demand of the Gospel.

Further, Cone's ecclesiology challenges the church with what it is called to become: a reconciled and restored community that transcends race, gender and social, strata. The main difference between King's beloved community and Cone's community of the oppressed has to do with the point of departure. Although Cone's community of the oppressed is inclusive of Black and white people, its location is in the Black community, because the Black community for Cone best symbolizes the contemporary Christ. The challenge facing other communities is to join Christ in this community. Membership in this community involves identity with victims, combined with an acknowledgment of the Oppressed One, Jesus of Nazareth. King would not be as careful concerning the location of the community. The beloved community, unlike the community of the oppressed, transcends location. In a profound sense, the beloved community is everywhere.

Even though the church's identity and the church's relevance to the world cannot be separated, Cone, nonetheless, insists that theology should not result in an accommodation to culture but in the liberation of culture. Here, theology becomes a cultural event: on the one hand, it is a part of the culture, yet on the other hand, it transcends the culture by calling the cultural ethos into question. This becomes possible for Black theology as the people's story is placed in dialogue with the biblical story and the people discover that the central theme that emerges in both instances is the theme of liberation. Thus the people are able to retrieve their past because they are set free in relation to that past, being able to free themselves for the first time with their own story.

Sometimes when King preaches to Black audiences he is able to tap the rich cultural resources and place them in conversation with the biblical text. Then the people through call and response witness to the freeing power of their own story in tandem with the biblical story. But King does not do this as well in some of his academic writing. His dissertation is a case in point, and it leads some scholars to be confused as to what his theological roots are. It is precisely at this point I believe that King would have benefited greatly if he had had the opportunity to be in dialogue with James Cone. Cone would have helped King to be more intentional in articulating and delineating his sources and to practice theological consistency, which is one of the marks of Cone's work. King benefited from a dialogue with Tillich and Barth, both white theologians, and many other theologians whom he cites with approbation throughout his work. But many of these theologians did not share an identity with his culture, and because of this, often in King's books, the fullness of the people's stories does not come through. For King to have been in dialogue with Black theologians would have helped in this direction. Perhaps something of the magnitude of the conversion that occurred at Morehouse when he met Benjamin Mays and George Kelsey would have happened again if he had had the opportunity to dialogue with James Cone.

But what we miss in book-length manuscripts, we regain in shorter manuscripts and in King's sermons and speeches. We must remember, however, that King was not a regular theologian (according to Karl Barth) and so was not primarily interested in theological consistency but like Athanasius and Martin Luther related the gospel to the situation at hand. King sought to relate Christian faith to the existential situation and to the world at large.

Both Cone and King came to understand faith as obedience to God's will. As King would often say: "I only want to do God's will." So for them, theology is an act of faith. What we may believe cannot be separated from what must be done to create the reconciled and restored community. Faith is more than correct belief; it is also a way of acting and thinking in the church and world. But faith is not enough: faith needs analysis because faith needs to understand the context of its action. Although revelation may be the content of faith, faith's context is not given in revelation. This means that it is not enough to exegete Scripture—the theologian must also exegete society. We see King exegeting both the biblical text and the contemporary context in his "Beyond Vietnam" speech and also in his "Letter from Birmingham Jail."

Another point of contact between King and Cone concerns their doctrines of sin. Sin is not a private and individualistic transgression that can be cured by an individual's act of repentance, leaving unchallenged the social order in which we live. Sin is both personal and social. The tendency to accentuate the private and personal dimension of sin tends to ignore the social and historical aspect of sin, which is expressed in oppressive structures and the exploitation of people and their domination by institutions and groups. The private view of sin often obfuscates the need for gender, class, and race analysis aimed at the restoration and reconciliation of broken communities. Christian theology has to take seriously the principalities and powers and the manifestation of wickedness in high places. To ignore this view of sin is to be unaware of the social-cosmic dimension of sin.

So for both Cone and King, sin builds up corporate structures of alienation and oppression that a person may not be able to overcome as an individual. Therefore liberation and reconciliation require participation in political organizations and processes (such as SCLC) that are geared at the destruction of systems of injustice and poverty. This then holds out the possibility of theology becoming a way of working for the liberation of God's creation with the confidence that God works with us.

5 MARTIN LUTHER KING JR.'S THEOLOGICAL PERSPECTIVE

A reading of the sermons, speeches, and books of Martin Luther King Jr. indicates a rough outline of the methods of Karl Barth, Paul Tillich, and James Cone—and an attempt to go further. King was not a scientific theologian and so had no keen interest in the systematic interpretation of the Christian faith for his and succeeding generations. It is clear, however, that in his attempt to relate the Christian faith to the struggles of oppressed people, we see glimpses of Barth's dialectical method, Tillich's method of correlation, and Cone's theology of the Black experience. King was not, like these theologians, overly concerned about method in theology for the sake of articulating a theological system. He allowed theology to serve the needs of the church and to provide the basis for leading oppressed people out of bondage.

King's letter from the Birmingham jail calls to mind Barth's theological method and determination that the task of theology is not to confirm and affirm church practice and proclamation but rather to criticize and revise church practice and proclamation. The anger of Barth's early writing and certainly the rage of the eighth-century B.C. prophets seem to inform King's theological response to a church and its leaders that called on him not to cause any trouble in his attempt to lead the oppressed out of the bondage of injustice.

In King's theological response to injustice and to a church that took sides with the status quo, we see an attempt to relate the biblical tradition to the present situation so that the injustice done to the poor by both unjust laws and the church's complicity in racism and structural injustice is exposed. Not only does King expose the church's complicity in racism and structural injustice in the society but the church is challenged to do justice and Christian faith becomes a struggle against exploitation and oppression of all sorts. In this letter it becomes clear that for Martin Luther King Jr., the moral task of the theologian becomes the proclamation of the dominion of God and the struggle in history to make it a present reality. King writes to the church from prison:

I am in Birmingham because injustice is here. Just as the prophets of the eighth century B.C. *left their villages and carried their "thus saith the Lord" far beyond the boundaries of their hometowns, and just as the Apostle Paul left his village of Tarsus and carried the gospel of Jesus Christ to the far corners of the Greco-Roman world, so I am compelled to carry the gospel of freedom beyond my own hometown. We know through painful experience that freedom is never voluntarily given by the oppressor; it must be demanded by the oppressed. Frankly, I have yet to engage in a direct-action campaign that was "well timed" in the view of those who have not suffered unduly from the disease of segregation. For years now I have heard the word "wait!" It rings in the ear of every Negro with piercing familiarity. This "wait" has almost always meant "Never."* [1]

Barth, like King, gave a great deal of time to prisoners and sought every opportunity to preach the gospel to them, and like King he would break unjust laws for the sake of the gospel. But King went beyond Barth in that his theological focus was praxis oriented. There was a theological commitment from King to practice theology from within the struggle to make the beloved community a present reality. It is the attempt by King to do theology from within the struggle to eke out a measure of dignity and self-respect for the exploited and victimized that calls attention to the difference in theological approaches. King illustrates the difference for us: "But when you have seen vicious mobs lynch your mothers and fathers at will and drown your sisters and brothers at whim; when you have seen hate filled policemen curse, kick and even kill your black brothers and sisters; when you see the vast majority of your twenty million Negro brothers smothering in an airtight cage of poverty in the midst of an affluent society."[2] It is the attempt to do theology in this context, to allow the divine law to call into question the injustice in the society, that points to the praxeological cutting edge of King's theology.

There are also points of contact between King's and Tillich's approaches to theology. King's attempt to do the truth in solidarity with victims calls attention to the primacy of praxis and the contextual character of his theology. King describes his commitment to the situation and the importance of a covenantal theology in this way:

We will have to repent in this generation not merely for the hateful words and actions of the bad people but for the appalling silence of the good people. Human progress never rolls in on the wheels of inevitability; it comes through the tireless efforts of men willing to be co-workers with God, and without their hard work, time itself becomes an ally of the forces of stagnation. We must use time creatively, in the knowledge that time is always ripe to do right. Now is the time to make real the promise of democracy and transform our pending national elegy into a creative psalm of brotherhood. Now is the time to lift our national policy from the quicksand of racial injustice to the solid rock of human dignity.[3]

It is King's commitment to do theology from the existential situation that indicates the congruency between King's and Tillich's theological approaches. Whereas Tillich focuses on ontological questions that arise from the universal situation, King highlights existential questions in the particular situation. This is not to say that Tillich's universal does not quest for the particular or that the existential does not have ontological significance for King but that the point of departure for King is concrete/historical whereas in Tillich's case it was ontological/universal.

This tendency of Tillich to focus on the human situation in general made him deal with broad categories such as alienation and estrangement, often without giving them sociological concreteness. Even if one admits that in his books *Love, Power, and Justice* and *The Courage to Be,* Tillich hints in the direction of sociological concreteness, one has to further admit that unlike King, Tillich's theology is predicated on the viability of the present socioeconomic system. Tillich's *Systematic Theology* does not begin with the need to change America. He seeks to relate Bible, tradition, and history with culture as most good theologians do, without giving us a revolutionary principle to help us question oppression in a theological way. Tillich's theology is colored by his theological perspective, and in essence he deals with questions that emerge from the general situation and seeks to shape his answers according to that situation. This in part may account for Tillich's silence on the struggle of the civil rights movement for justice and freedom in America. This may seem surprising since the economic, political, and theological foundation of America was shaken by the civil rights movement. Tillich lectured in the midst of the revolution without speaking a word in reference to that revolution.

How may we understand Tillich's silence? Is it attributable to his method? May we acknowledge that perhaps Tillich's method does not go far enough? May we learn from King that as an American theologian it is not enough to correlate message and existence, human question and divine answer, but that message and existence must be given sociological concreteness. That is, theology must deal with Black existence and white existence, racism, sexism, and the multiforms of exploitation that the victims of exploitation face. Further, we must urge that theology becomes revolutionary activity. It must set out to change the world. King gives a praxeological focus to theology:

> *In own our nation another unjust and evil system,*
> *known as segregation, for nearly one hundred years inflicted*
> *the Negro with a sense of inferiority, deprived him of his*
> *personhood, and denied him his birthright of life, liberty,*
> *and the pursuit of happiness. Segregation has been the*
> *Negro's burden and America's shame. . . . Today we know*
> *with certainty that segregation is dead. . . . When in future*
> *generations men look back upon these turbulent, tension*
> *packed days through which we are passing, they will see*
> *God working through history for the salvation of man. They*
> *will know that God was working through those men who had*
> *the vision to perceive that no nation could survive half slave*
> *and half free. God is able to conquer the evils of history.*[4]

When theologians begin to see the world from this perspective, theology becomes revolutionary activity. It was the perceived failure of Tillich to give sociological concreteness to God-talk that led Martin King in his dissertation for Boston University to charge Tillich with being abstruse and abstract in his attempt to relate God to the evil in our world. According to King, Tillich attributes the evil in the world to some nonrational aspect of God's nature and thereby introduces a dualism into the divine nature, which he finds unsatisfactory. Hence he concludes that Tillich's view of God suffers from metaphysical dualism: "Tillich leaves such a tremendous gap between God as *abyss* and God as *logos* that there hardly appears to be a point of contact between the two. . . . So great is the mystery between *abyss* and *logos* that one is compelled to wonder why the two should be called God."[5]

King would have chafed at the term *Black theology,* as James Cone used it. Once we get beyond the labels of Black theology and Black power, however, there are striking similarities between the approaches of Cone and King to theology. Both theologians seek to relate the gospel of Jesus to the existential situation; and they assert a Christological focus in their attempts to relate the gospel to situations in which people hurt and are humiliated. Further there is a theological commitment from both theologians to translate the gospel of Jesus as commitment not only for personal but also social change. This correspondence of views should not surprise us as both are sons of the Black church and served as pastors and theologians in that church. The central difference between both approaches has to do with liberation being the hermeneutical key for Cone and reconciliation being that key for King.

MAPPING THE JOURNEY

As early as 1956, King attempted to relate the gospel to the existential situation. The scenario was the city of Montgomery's response to Black people, who had practically closed down the city bus line in a refusal to ride the buses following the arrest of Mrs. Rosa Parks, who refused to sit in the back of the bus. The mayor of Montgomery called a meeting of his citizens' committee, along with members of the Montgomery City Bus Line, to meet with the Montgomery Improvement Association, led by Martin Luther King Jr. Members of the mayor's delegation included the Reverend Henry Parker, the pastor of First Baptist Church; the Reverend E. Stanley Frazier, minister of St. James Methodist Church; and the Reverend Henry Russel of Trinity Presbyterian Church.

King points out that it did not take long for the meeting to come to an impasse, because both the mayor's committee and officials from the bus company refused to grant the modest requests of the Black community for: (a) a guarantee of courteous treatment when they ride the buses; (b) passengers to be seated on a first-come, first-served basis, the Negroes seating from the back; and (c) the employment of Black bus operators on predominantly Black routes. The mayor's committee and officials from the bus company would not hear of the request for Black people to be employed as bus operators. And so the Montgomery Improvement Association modified this modest request, asking instead that the bus company take applications of Blacks for possible vacancies that may occur in the future.

It was at this point in their meeting that the Reverend Dr. Frazier, "one of the most outspoken segregationists in the Methodist Church,"[6] made it clear that according to his reading of the Scriptures, Black people were wrong in boycotting the buses. According to Dr. Frazier, it was even more shameful that the boycott against the buses were led by ministers of the gospel. Commenting on Frazier's remarks, King reports:

He made it clear . . . that the job of the minister . . . is to lead the souls of men to God, not to bring about confusion by getting tangled up in transitory social problems. He moved on to a brief discussion of the Christmas story. In evocative terms he talked of "God's unspeakable gift." He ended by saying that as we moved into the Christmas season our hearts and minds should be turned toward the Babe of Bethlehem; and he urged the Negro ministers to leave the meeting determined to bring this boycott to a close and lead their people instead "to a glorious experience of the Christian faith."[7]

Needless to say, King instructed the good Dr. Frazier and the mayor's delegation that they were no strangers to the gospel of Jesus Christ. King explains:

We too know the Jesus that the minister just referred to. . . . We have had an experience with him, and we believe firmly in the revelation of God in Jesus Christ. I can see no conflict between our devotion to Jesus Christ and our present action. In fact I see a necessary relationship. If one is truly devoted to the religion of Jesus he will seek to rid the world of social evils. The gospel is social as well as personal.[8]

So as early as 1956, Martin King began to make the connection between the gospel of Jesus Christ and the existential predicament of Black people. There was an indissoluble connection between the gospel of Jesus and the community of the oppressed. He discovered that the gospel was social as well as personal. This attempt to live with two warrants at once—the personal and social gospel—is what made the distinctive difference between his approach to the gospel and the other pastors.

These double warrants are thematic of King's work. He insisted that the Christian faith had to address problems of politics, which for economic and social reasons blight the life of God's children. In his Letter from Birmingham Jail, King points out that the gospel of Jesus Christ makes it clear that situations where there is no freedom are contexts that must be broken through for Christ's sake. The church cannot any longer be content to coexist with any form of economic and social oppression A commitment to personal salvation must mean at the same time a commitment to social-structural change. Correct beliefs must not be separated from correct action. In an assessment of the early years of the civil rights movement, King states:

> From the beginning a basic philosophy guided the movement. The guiding principle has since been referred to variously as non-violent resistance, noncooperation, and passive resistance. But in the first days of the protest none of these expressions was mentioned; the phrase most often heard was "Christian love." It was the Sermon on the Mount, rather than a doctrine of passive resistance, that initially inspired the Negroes of Montgomery to dignified social action. It was Jesus of Nazareth that stirred the Negroes to protest with the creative weapon of love.[9]

The guiding principle was Christian love. There was no doubt in King's mind that Christian faith required the combining of a deeply religious faith with an intense social involvement. He refused to separate the religious and the ethical, the spiritual and the secular, and the personal and the social.

This theological commitment for the liberation of his people antedates the formation of the Montgomery Improvement Association. During his first year as pastor of the Dexter Avenue Baptist

Church, King organized a Social and Political Action Commission as a critical instrument for liberation at the church. This commission had a number of functions: (a) to keep the membership of the congregation informed concerning the social, political, and economic situation in Montgomery; (b) to encourage the registration of voters and to educate them concerning the issues that were pertinent to the liberation of the oppressed. The congregation was also encouraged through this channel to join humanistic agencies that were committed to the elevation and liberation of the Black race, and finally; (c) this committee was charged to empower and involve the congregation in civic and social issues in the community.[10] In *Pilgrimage to Nonviolence,* King describes this integration of spiritual and physical in religion:

> *The gospel at its best deals with the whole man, not only with his soul but also his body, not only his spiritual well-being but also his material well-being. A religion that professes a concern for the souls of men and is not equally concerned about the slums that damn them, the economic conditions that strangle them, and the social conditions that cripple them, is a spiritually moribund religion.*[11]

RECONCILIATION THE MAIN KEY

The theologion Cone postulates liberation as the main key that unlocks Scripture and at the same time provides the frame of reference for social criticism; for King, the key is reconciliation. The theme of reconciliation is the main key in which the struggle for freedom is cast. Sometimes he speaks of the goal of the struggle as integration, at other times as the creation of the beloved community: but all the time he is referring to reconciliation.

Reconciliation is a theological commitment for King. The theological underpinning for this understanding of reconciliation is the notion of an inclusive covenant made possible by God's gift of the *imago dei.* King calls attention to this thrust in his work when on the eve of the Black citizens of Montgomery's return to the buses, he counseled them not to rejoice "over our white brothers," but to "act in such a way as to make possible a coming together of white people and colored people on the basis of real harmony of interests and understanding. . . . As we go back to the buses let us be loving enough to turn an enemy into a friend. We must move from protest to reconciliation. It is my firm conviction that God is working in Montgomery."[12]

This fundamental confidence that God was at work in Montgomery provided the basis for King's insistence that enemies should become friends and that Black people and white people should put their differences aside and move from protest to reconciliation. This challenge to the community to move from protest to reconciliation was based on an understanding that human beings belong to a moral community rooted in an inclusive covenant. Each person matters in the community in her or his own right, because the divine life pulsates in her/his heart. Because God is intimately involved in the struggle of God's people in the community, reconciliation is not merely an eschatological but a historical possibility. King puts it this way:

We can remember days when unfavorable court decisions came upon us like tidal waves, leaving us treading the waters of despair. But amid all of this we have kept going with the faith that as we struggle, God struggles with us, and that the arc of the moral universe, although long, is bending toward justice. We have lived under the agony and darkness of Good Friday with the conviction that one day the heightened glow of Easter would emerge on the horizon. We have seen truth crucified and goodness buried, but we have kept going with the conviction that truth crushed to the ground will rise again.[13]

It was this theological commitment to reconciliation as a goal for community that made violence as a means for change unacceptable. Nonviolence was a logical obligation that King felt regarding reconciliation as a goal for the building of community. According to King, destructive means cannot portend toward constructive ends.

Both means and ends must reflect a commitment to reconciliation. Constructive ends require constructive means: "The end of violence or the aftermath of violence is bitterness. The aftermath of non-violence is reconciliation and the creation of the beloved community. A boycott is never an end within itself. It is merely a means to awaken a sense of shame within the oppressor but the end is reconciliation, the end is redemption."[14] Persons must be treated as ends in themselves and never as means and be willing to lose themselves for the good of the community in order to find themselves.

KING'S DOCTRINE OF GOD

King's confidence in reconciliation was based not only on the presupposition of an inclusive covenant but also in his profound trust in a personal God. The universe he claimed is under the control of a loving God who offers cosmic companionship in the struggle for righteousness. King articulates for us his faith in a personal God:

The agonizing moments through which I have passed during the last few years have also drawn me closer to God. More than ever before I am convinced of the reality of a personal God. True, I have always believed in the personality of God. But in the past the idea of a personal God was little more than a metaphysical category that I found theologically and philosophically satisfying. Now it is a living reality that has been validated in the experiences of every day life. God has been profoundly real to me in recent years.[15]

There are two important corollaries to this understanding of a personal God. Because there is a personal God, there is a natural moral order to the universe. Further, this God is involved in the stuff of history. This belief that there is a moral order in the universe was learned by King in the Black church and later reinforced at Crozer Theological Seminary and Boston University. This moral order in the universe is rooted in the nature of God. A God without moral concern may be all powerful and all knowing but would not be the object of faith. God is at the core and the heartbeat of the cosmos: "It reminds us that the universe is on the side of justice. It says to those who struggle for justice; 'you do not struggle alone, but God struggles with you.' This belief that God is on the side of truth and justice comes down to us from the long tradition of our Christian faith."[16]

The conviction that there are divine laws just as there are physical laws at the heart of the universe constitutes the essence of King's life and thought. History he claimed is bound by a divine purpose. The world is not a child of chance but has both its genesis and its goal in God. Good Friday may occupy the throne for a time but ultimately it must give way to the triumphant drum beats of Easter. This indomitable confidence in the goodness of God made King very sure that social, economic, and political manifestations of evil had no permanent basis in reality. This evil age, he claimed, is on its way out and God's new age of peace is on its way in. This new age, however, does not come in on the wheels of inevitability. The church is called to join God in the task of making the new age a reality. God needs human agents in the creation of a new moral order. We bring in this new order "not through violence; not through hate; no, not even through boycotts; but through love. . . . But we must remember as we boycott that a boycott is not an end within itself; . . . the end is reconciliation; the end is redemption; the end is the creation of the beloved community."[17]

King was insistent that if oppressed people would join God in the task of bringing in the beloved community, they could defeat the principalities and the powers of racism, materialism, and militarism. He argued that the victory in Montgomery was not made possible by creative leadership or the fact that Black people could not take the atrocities meted out to them any longer. The secret lay in the presence of a personal God at the center of the universe. King writes:

So every rational explanation breaks down at some
point. There is something about the protest that is
suprarational; it cannot be explained without a divine
dimension. Some may call it a principle of concretion, with

*Alfred N. Whitehead; or a process of integration, with
Henry N. Weiman; or Being-itself, with Paul Tillich; or a
personal God. Whatever the name, some extra-human force
labors to create a harmony out of the discords of the
universe. There is a creative force that works to pull down
mountains of evil and level hilltops of injustice. God still
works through history his wonders to perform.*[18]

For King, however, this personal God at the core of the universe does not lead to notions of privatization and individualism but rather challenges us to commit to the community and a world perspective. King's doctrine of reconciliation encompasses a world vision. King would often remind us that one of the consequences of the technological age is that the world has become a neighborhood. The personal God at the heart of the universe confronts us with the ethical commitment to make our world a human community. King writes: "We must all learn to live together as brothers, or we will all perish as fools. We are tied together in the single garment of destiny, caught in an inescapable network of mutuality. And whatever affects one directly affects all indirectly. . . . This is the way God's universe is made; this is the way it is structured."[19]

King links his belief in the moral law of the cosmos with the cross of Christ, the supreme manifestation of love. For King, the cross of Christ functions as a telescope through which the love of God is mediated: "The cross is the eternal expression of the length to which God will go in order to restore broken community. The resurrection is a symbol of God's triumph over all the forces that seek to block community. The Holy Spirit is the continuing community creating reality that moves through history."[20] The love of God manifested in the cross of Christ requires social justice as a basis for authentic community. Because of this, human rights for those on the margins of society could not be ignored or manipulated by unscrupulous people. Rather, basic human rights for the poor constitute a theological and moral baseline for the community. Harold DeWolf, with whom King wrote his doctoral dissertation, comments on King's use of the cross of Christ:

The way of the cross by which we are saved is no mere accepting of certain beliefs nor is the salvation only for another world. To walk in the way of the cross is to give oneself for love and justice, to account one's life as expendable for the sake of fulfilling the need of others, to suffer violence and never return to it.[21]

It is the love of God as expressed in the cross of Christ that provides the glue that holds communities together. This love of God as the power of reconciliation unites races and fractured communities. This love provides the commitment to struggle against segregation and all that would threaten the wholeness of community. His commitment to this love of God manifested in the cross of Christ made King insist that the struggle was not against persons or groups but against structures of social evil and the forces of evil itself, which seek to fragment the community. The power of love that issues forth in reconciliation precludes an attack on persons or groups but rather seeks to overcome evil and thereby free people for community: "We meet the forces of hate with the power of love; we meet physical force with soul force."

Another consequence of King's doctrine of God was his belief that God was active in history. This confidence in the divine activity in history is related to the notion of a personal God who is the heartbeat of the universe. The God who is at the core of the universe is not only transcendent to the world but immanent. This God "is not outside the world looking on with a cold sort of indifference. Here on all the roads of life, he is striving in our striving. Like an ever loving Father, he is working through history for the salvation of his children."[22] The creator is the divine participant. God participates in the struggles of God's people. This means that the civil rights movement was not merely a struggle of the oppressed against the status quo but more important the historic struggle of good against evil. The struggle against segregation and poverty was the struggle of

God against the forces of evil. It is within history that we experience the power of God that defeats evil.

Being shaped by the Black church, King gave great importance to the Exodus story as God's deliverance of Israel from slavery and oppression. He saw a parallel between Israel's story of oppression and that of Black people in America. There were lessons Black people had to learn from Pharaoh's Egypt. One lesson is that freedom is never offered as a gift. Freedom is never won without struggle and the struggle is never primarily against persons but against the vicious systems and structures that would deny God's children their freedom. King compares the historical circumstances of the civil rights movement with Israel's situation in Egypt:

Looking back, we see the forces of segregation gradually dying on the seashore. The problem is far from solved and gigantic mountains of opposition lie ahead, but at least we have left Egypt, and with patient yet firm determination we shall reach the promised land. Evil in the form of injustice and exploitation shall not survive forever. A Red Sea passage in history ultimately brings the forces of goodness to victory, and the closing of the same waters mark the doom and the destruction of the forces of evil. All this reminds us that evil carries the seed of its own destruction. In the long run right defeated is stronger than evil triumphant.[23]

The dominion of God provides an opening in history. The reality of existing evil in history does not destroy the confidence in the liberating possibilities of the divine involvement in history. This is so because the dominion of God witnesses both to an *already* but also to a *not yet*. The presence of the dominion of God in history points to a new future and a new history that the divine activity makes possible. King writes:

The kingdom of God as a universal is not yet. *Because sin exists on every level of man's existence, the death of one tyranny is followed by the emergence of another*

tyranny. . . . Even though all progress is precarious, within
limits real social progress may be made. . . . And though the
kingdom of God may remain not yet *as a universal reality in*
history, in the present it may exist in such isolated forms as
in judgement, in personal devotion, and in some group life.[24]

The *not yet* does not rob the present of the assurance of divine activity in the present. On the contrary, eschatology becomes history as the victims of oppression become participants of the dominion as they struggle for the *novum* in history. This dynamic understanding of history provided for King a revolutionary principle that opened up the possibility of changing the face of American society. Although sometimes evil may seem to be in the ascendancy, there is a checkpoint in history. Such a checkpoint was demonstrated in the confrontation between Moses and Pharaoh and in the ensuing conflict between the Israelites and the Egyptians. The presence of God in history ensured the destruction of Egyptian bondage, which could not prevail against God's will. Many people came to share King's confidence in the possibility of the *novum* breaking in history, and so King was regarded as a modern Moses. Attributing the Negro spiritual to King they would sing:

Go down, Moses
Go down to Egypt land
Go tell ol' Pharaoh
Let my people go.

But King was enough of a Baptist preacher not only to talk about the relationship of the *already* and the *not yet* in history but in sermonic style to talk about the final eschaton and how the God who is in history transcends history and thereby judges history. According to King, the vision of the God who judges history places ethical responsibility on human beings to practice justice and reconciliation in history. It will not be enough for us to recite a catalog of scientific achievements. Technological and scientific accomplishments will not impress the God who judges history. This God will judge us by our actions on behalf of the victims of oppression and by our commitment to restore broken community. A signal of our commitment to reconciliation would mean among other things a willingness to abolish war and affirm the sanctity and dignity of all God's children: "One day we will have to stand before the God of history" writes King, "and we will talk in terms of the things we have done. Yes we will be able to say we built gargantuan bridges to span the seas. . . . It seems that I can hear the God of history saying, 'That was not enough! But I was hungry and you fed me not.'"[25]

Our hope as a people is in John's vision on the isle of Patmos of a new Jerusalem descending out of heaven from the God who said, "Behold, I make all things new—former things are passed away." It is as the oppressed claim this vision and become participants in the creation of the new humanity that God's new day of justice and authentic community will emerge.

KING'S DOCTRINE OF HUMANITY

King's doctrine of humanity is an outgrowth of his doctrine of God. The sacredness of human personality was a constant theme in speeches and sermons. Every human being by virtue of being human has inherent worth, and no person, society, or culture has the right to deny his/her personhood. One of the sins against humanity is the attempt of people in power to strip the oppressed of their freedom and dignity. This is what makes segregation, racism, poverty, and war sins against God. King writes: "The essence of man is found in freedom. This is what Paul Tillich means when he declares, 'Man is man because he is free,' or what Tolstoy implies when he says, 'I cannot conceive of a man not being free unless he is dead.'"[26] King learned from Tillich that any meaningful attempt to discuss the nature and destiny of humanity must include a discussion of freedom.

King contends that freedom should not be understood as freedom of the will because the will is only one function or one faculty of the self. To talk further about the freedom of the will is an abstraction. It makes the will an object and thus destroys the unity of freedom. A centered self includes both subject and object and needs this unity to be free. Since freedom may not be defined in terms of the will, we must ask, what then is freedom? According to King, there are three moments in the life of freedom: (1) To be free is to be able to deliberate. That means one ought to be able to weigh alternatives. (2) To be free is to be in a position to make decisions. The capacity to make decisions that affect one's destiny is the hallmark of freedom. One must be able to say yes or no. "A decision is an incision." And finally, (3) To be free is to be responsible. Freedom means taking responsibility for one's action. And we cannot take responsibility for actions if we are denied our choices.[27]

Therefore, to be free is to be human and to be human is to be free. It is here that King speaks of sin as anything that violates one's freedom. The absence of freedom is the negation of personhood. To be unable to choose where one will live, or go to school, or how one will survive is to relegate one to a form of existence that is not worthy of human beings. It is this denial of freedom to the oppressed that makes Martin King speak of racism and segregation as "social leprosy." To deny one's basic human right to life, liberty, and the pursuit of happiness on the basis of race, gender, or class is to take away that person's capacity to be responsible, to decide, and to deliberate.

There is an ontological grounding for King's attempt to talk about the worth of human beings. The basis for human freedom is rooted in the sanctity of personality. Every person is worthy of respect because God loves him or her: "The worth of an individual does not lie in the measure of his intellect, his racial origin, or social position. Human worth lies in relatedness to God. An individual has value because he has value to God."[28]

King anchors this view of the worth of persons in the biblical and theological understanding of the image of God. Because God's grace is the basis of the worth of human beings, it means that all persons are of equal worth. There is no theological or biblical basis for regarding Western people as superior to other peoples or for regarding white people as superior to Black people. The image of God is universally shared in an equal way by all persons. Every human being has stamped in his/her personality the indelible image of God. King states succinctly:

> *Our Hebraic-Christian tradition refers to this inherent dignity of man in the Biblical term* the image of God. *This innate worth referred to in the phrase the image of God is universally shared in equal portions by all men. There is no graded scale of essential worth; there is no divine right of one race which differs from the divine right of another. Every human being has etched in his personality the indelible stamp of the creator.*[29]

Failure to view persons in the light of the *image of God* is to reduce them to the status of things—to fall in the trap of treating persons as means rather than ends in themselves. King borrows Martin Buber's phrase and speaks of reducing persons to an "I-it" relationship: "The tragedy of segregation is that it treats men as means rather than ends, and thereby reduces them to things rather than persons. . . . Segregation substitutes an 'I-it' relationship for an 'I-thou' relationship."[30]

King differentiates between the physical and the spiritual qualities of freedom. The physical dimension of freedom is protected by law enforcement agencies and this should not blur the mind to the unenforceable quality of freedom. The higher law, so to speak, is the law of love. Love as the spiritual quality of freedom points to the unenforceable. Love cannot be demanded—it must be awakened: "No code of conduct ever compelled a father to love his children or a husband to show affection to his wife. The law court may force him to provide bread for the family, but it cannot make him provide the bread of love. A good father is obedient to the unenforceable."[31] The unenforceable points to the spiritual dimension of freedom. We may obey the law for love's sake, and conversely, we may break the law for love's sake.

While asserting the importance of law enforcement to secure basic human rights for the oppressed, King nonetheless affirms the importance of recognizing the higher law, the divine law, which calls all human laws into question. He speaks of the necessity of love:

> A vigorous enforcement of civil rights will bring an end
> to segregated public facilities which are barriers to a truly
> desegregated society, but it cannot bring an end to fears,
> prejudice, pride, and the irrationality, which are the barriers
> to a truly integrated society. Those dark and demonic
> responses will be removed only as men are possessed by the
> invisible, inner law which etches on their hearts the
> conviction that all men are brothers and that love is
> mankind's most potent weapon for personal and social
> transformation.[32]

It is with love as soul force that the oppressed will be able to match physical force. King often spoke of love for self, neighbor, and God as "the three dimensions of the complete life." It was very clear to King, however, that self-love should be subordinate to love for neighbor. Like the Good Samaritan, we are called to risk life for neighbor. In his sermon "On Being a Good Neighbor," King speaks of love as dangerous altruism, which aids us on the journey towards reconciliation. This love refuses to categorize people in terms of Jew or Gentile, Russian or American, Black or white. With the Good Samaritan as our role model we are called to look beyond the accident of race, religion, and nationality and consider people as our brothers and sisters. It is at the level of solidarity that we will move beyond pity for those in trouble on the Jericho road and share their pain and anguish in a willingness to do more than duty demands.

It is this commitment to reconciliation that will allow us to put the needs of our neighbors at the forefront, as we seek to restore communities that are fractured. According to King, the death of Christ at Calvary was a sacrificial act that not only transcended race, creed, class, and nationality but was both dangerous and excessive: "In our quest to make neighborly love a reality, we have, in addition to the inspiring example of the Good Samaritan, the magnanimous life of our Christ to guide us. . . . His altruism was excessive, for he chose to die on calvary."[33] In his Nobel Prize acceptance speech, King speaks of hate and self-centeredness giving way to egalitarian love: "I believe that what self-centered men have torn down men other-centered can build up. I still believe that one day mankind will bow before the altars of God and be crowned triumphant over war and bloodshed, and nonviolent redemptive good will proclaim the rule of the land."[34] In this reconciling community that King envisions, "The lion and the lamb shall lie down together and every man shall sit down under his own vine and fig tree and none shall be afraid."[35]

This love that is at the center of the reconciling community also asks concerning the circumstances that shape human existence. Love does this by insisting that justice be done in human relationships, because justice cannot be separated from love. Indeed, justice is not the antithesis of love but constitutes its inner meaning. Love and justice force us to inquire concerning how power functions in the community. To attempt to separate love, power, and justice is to be guilty of a faulty analysis of the human situation: "Power at its best is love implementing the demands of justice, and justice at its best is power correcting everything that stands against love."[36]

Historically, from the plantations in the South to the ghettoes in the North, Black people have been voiceless and powerless. They have been unable to make decisions that affect their lives and destinies. Black people have not had the power to effect meaningful changes in the way they live. The absence of power means that they cannot be held responsible for their crimes, because these crimes have been derivative. They lack the power to change the system that crushes them. Speaking of the loss of power that is emblematic of life in the Black community, King writes:

The plantation and the ghetto were created by those who had power, both to confine those who had no power and to perpetuate their powerlessness. The problem of transforming the ghetto, therefore, is a problem of power-

confrontation of the forces of power demanding change and the forces of power dedicated to preserving the status quo. Now power properly understood is nothing but the ability to achieve purpose. It is the strength required to bring about social, political and economic change.[37]

Love provides a moral horizon for power. Power without love is reckless and love without power is anemic. When love is joined with power they demand justice. Love, power, and justice demand a restructuring of American society in such a way that barriers to equality are removed and the atmosphere for reconciliation is created. This restructuring of the society that love, power, and justice demand implies that part of the answer to our dilemma is found neither in capitalism nor in communism but in a reconciling community of sisterhood and brotherhood shaped by the reign of God. Love, power, and justice demand, "America, you must be born again."[38] That is, the whole structure must be changed.

King often reminds us: "It's all right to talk about 'long white robes over yonder,' in all of its symbolism. But ultimately people want some suits and dresses and shoes to wear down here. It's all right to talk about 'streets flowing with milk and honey,' but God has commanded us to be concerned about the slums down here, and his children who can't eat three square meals a day."[39] Talk about the new Jerusalem should be at the same time a commitment to work for a new Atlanta, a new Philadelphia, a new Los Angeles. The call for reconciliation must be at the same time a call for economic justice. This call to economic justice includes the development of Black-owned businesses and a commitment to be industrious as oppressed people insist on self-help and self-reliance. As the oppressed build their own businesses and establish self-help and self-reliance, they must be willing to withdraw economic support from Coca-Cola, Sealtest Milk, and Wonder Bread, which are not committed to treat all of God's children fairly.[40] The poor must build their own economic base. This is one way to combat the triplets of racism, economic exploitation, and war. King writes:

We've got to strengthen black institutions. I call upon you to take your money out of the banks downtown and deposit your money in Tri-State bank—we want a "bank-in" movement in Memphis. . . . You have six or seven black insurance companies in Memphis. Take out your insurance there.[41]

Reconciliation for Martin King is between equals, not between an inferior and a superior. In order that all people may have dignity in their living circumstances, he calls for the destruction of slums and for the providing of jobs for everyone: "We are demanding an emergency program to provide employment for everyone in need of a job, or if a work program is impracticable, a guaranteed annual income at levels that sustain life in decent circumstances."[42]

Theology has to be done in the life situation. A right relationship with God means a holy impatience with the present order in which people are denied their dignity. The vision of the restored and reconciled community makes it impossible to accept reality as it is. With unprecedented passion, King underscores his commitment to work for the restored and reconciled community:

I cannot forget that the Nobel Prize for Peace was also a commission—a commission to work harder for "the brotherhood of man." This is a calling which takes me beyond national allegiances, but even if it were not present, I would have to live with the meaning of my commitment to the ministry of Jesus Christ. . . .

We are called to speak for the weak, for the voiceless, for the victims of our nation, and for those it calls enemy, for no document from human hands can make these humans any less our brothers.[43]

The vision of the restored community cannot serve the purpose of postponing a confrontation with the realities of the present order; rather it asserts that commitment to Jesus Christ insists on change in social relationships and in the world at large. Reconciliation includes liberation.

The central issue for King concerns neither the articulation of the relationship between theology and philosophy, nor a discussion of the human and divine nature of Christ, but rather an attempt to grapple and ferret out an answer to the question, What does Christian faith require in an oppressive situation? There was no debate as to whether this faith would issue forth in personal conversion or structural conversion of the society. As a Baptist pastor, King believes in the necessity of personal conversion; and even if one argues that before 1965 he did not quite understand the endemic and systemic nature of social evil in America, it is clear that after the experience in Chicago in 1965, he began to call for structural change in the society. He understood the evil use of power as centered not merely in the will of individuals but as constitutive of the social arrangement of the society: "The slums are the handiwork of a vicious system of the white society; Negroes live in them, but do not make them, anymore than a prisoner makes a prison. . . . The white society, unprepared and unwilling to accept radical structural change, is resisting firmly and thus producing chaos because the force for change is vital and aggressive."[44]

King takes the issues that concern the poor—racism, poverty, and exploitation—and places them at the center of theological attention. Here reconciliation means more than integration; it means doing justice. Reconciliation includes liberation. King has modeled for us how to work for the reconciliation of all people, and at the same time to press for a removal of the causes that separate us. The goal of reconciliation was the salvation of all. This required more than a change of heart. Change was required in economics and politics. Change was required in the foundation of society.

SUMMARY

Martin King related the gospel of freedom to the conflict-ridden situation in which the oppressed yearned for the restored and reconciling community. So, for him, whether the oppressed exegeted Scripture or society, the central theme that emerged was love aiding us on the way to reconciliation.

In King's attempt to talk about what faith requires in a situation of oppression, we begin to understand the theological task:

1. The theologian must work from within the struggle to relate Christian faith to the concrete conditions that affect both body and soul. Further, Christian faith must become incarnational as the community embodies the life and teachings of Jesus of Nazareth. It is in this sense that Christ becomes normative for the faith and life of the community.

2. Commitment to the struggle to change the world and a willingness to lay down one's life in the struggle for justice must be the mark of the theologian. This means among other things that the concrete problems of the community must become grist for the theological mill. The problems of justice, poverty and powerlessness, and peace come to the center of theological concern.

3. Reconciliation becomes the main idea in which Christian theology is set. Reconciliation is not posited in a dialectical tension with liberation, but rather liberation becomes the motive force that empowers the community in its quest for a restored community.

The presupposition of the doctrine of reconciliation for King is the inclusive covenant that God has with all God's children and God's creation. This covenant requires that the means for liberation be consistent with the ends sought. Because the end sought is a restored and reconciled community, the only appropriate means for struggle is nonviolence. Nonviolence as a method of liberation that must aid us into reconciliation will ensure that enemies will be won as friends and that instruments of hate cannot serve the goals of love.

Because human freedom is anchored in divine freedom, salvation is assured because of the covenant between human beings and God. It is this covenantal theology that provides the hope for reconciliation. The central hope for King was a praxeological commitment to this covenant with God: "These deadly, paralyzing evils can be removed by a humanity perfectly united through obedience with God. Moral victory will come as God fills man and man opens his life by faith to God, even as the gulf opens to the overflowing waters of the river."[45] King was convinced that racial justice and the elimination of poverty was a distinct possibility in his time if human beings would allow God's will to become incarnate in their lives. God's freeing activity in history and the human response to God's freedom must become the hallmark of the journey into reconciliation.

Further, the theologian must join faith and praxis. The gospel of Jesus Christ must be related to the plight of those who suffer and are heavy laden in such a way that they discover that their quest for freedom is consistent with the biblical story of freedom. So whether or not victims listen to the biblical text or the contemporary context, the commitment to reconciliation remains the same.

The biblical text points to God's freeing activity in history and the contemporary context points to the yearning and groaning for freedom in the situation of exploitation and alienation. Whenever the oppressed open up themselves to God's will in their situation of oppression, "as the gulf opens to the overflowing waters of the river," God fills the human community with love, mutual respect, and understanding. And the goal of reconciliation will become a reality in our midst.

Emblematic of Dr. King's work was his advocacy and struggle for the eradication of oppression in its economic, social, and political manifestations. There was no doubt in King's mind that the revolutionary thrust of the gospel of love demanded the quest for justice. King came to understand that the oppressed needed more than integrated bathrooms and restaurants if they were to affirm their humanity as daughters and sons of God. He came to understand that change was required in the foundations of society—in its economic, social, and political spheres. This made King willing to challenge big business, its god of profit, and the unbridled greed that characterize a capitalist society. In the end he accepted a modified form of Black power and even wore a button that read, "Black is Beautiful."

What King hoped to achieve with the Poor People's March on Washington was a disruption of the oppressive structures of power. On the one hand he was critical of capitalism and on the other he was distrustful of communism. In *Where Do We Go from Here?*

Chaos or Community King writes: "We must honestly admit capitalism has often left a gulf between superfluous wealth and abject
poverty, has created conditions permitting necessities to be taken
from the many to give luxuries to the few. . . . Equally, Communism
reduces men to a cog in the wheel of the state. . . . Man is a means
to that end. He has no inalienable rights."[46]

We must go on, however, to affirm that as Jesus provided daily
bread and the restoration of the dignity of the oppressed, so as the
church faces the twenty-first century, it must deal with the multi-
form expressions of oppression. Because the church takes the claims
of the gospel of love seriously, it must continue the search for
economic justice, the struggle for human dignity and human rights
for all people, and the quest for the freedom of the human spirit.

One of the problems that the church faces is that often when it
preaches freedom in one area, it advocates bondage in another area.
Many devout church people do not see the gospel of love demanding
liberation in all areas of life. There are some churches that turn
inward in the search for faith and thereby neglect and ignore the
sociopolitical and economic dimensions of the gospel. For example,
in many churches the place of women is circumscribed. Women are
not free to participate in leadership roles at all levels. Even as
revolutionary a leader as Martin Luther King Jr. was a victim of the
patriarchal culture that shaped the society and the church in the
1950s and 1960s. Although the teaching of Jesus contains the openness to a new future for all God's children, King often gave in to
pressure from those around him to omit women from the ranks of
leadership in the organization that he led. In *Martin and Malcolm
and America,* James Cone writes:

> *Like most white and black men of the 1960s, their
> attitude toward women was shaped by their acceptance of
> patriarchal values as the norm for family and society.
> Following the pattern of white religious bodies, the Black
> church and the Nation of Islam provided religious
> justification for the subordination of women. While Martin
> and Malcolm challenged white values regarding race, their*

acceptance of black male privilege prevented them from seeing the connection between racism and sexism.[47]

The issue of the role of women in society and the church is larger than admitting that Martin Luther King Jr. was insensitive to sexism. The church itself contributed to the oppression of women in society by its attempt to keep women in subordinate roles. The challenge for the church is for renewal from within as it seeks to acknowledge the sovereignty of Christ.

CHAPTER 6

MARTIN LUTHER KING AND WOMANIST THEOLOGY

In *White Women's Christ and Black Women's Jesus,* Jacquelyn Grant points out that the oppression of women in the church and in society lead women to ask as their central question, "What has Jesus Christ to do with the status of women in the church and in society?" This question is a paraphrase of the question Jesus asked his disciples, "Who do you say that I am?" Grant indicates that for a long time men have sought to answer this question for women, but this must not continue, as women have to answer this question from their own experience. In the past, women have allowed men to say who Jesus is for them, thereby denying the validity of their own experience. The problem is not merely that men have suggested answers to this question but that they have sought to give definitive answers. Dr. Grant states the problem:

> *Since man is limited by his social context and interests, Jesus Christ has been defined within the narrow parameters of the male consciousness. That is to say, the social context of the men who have been theologizing has been the normative criterion upon which theological interpretations have been based. What this has meant is that Jesus Christ consistently has been used to give legitimacy to the customary beliefs regarding the status of women.*[1]

To ask what the church teaches about Jesus Christ is to inquire about Jesus from within the parameter of male consciousness. Grant reminds us that in A.D. 325 the church settled the question regarding Jesus' identity in relation to God by condemning Arianism. It was established that Jesus was of the same being as God. He was not of the created order, but of the same essence or substance as the father. However, the church had to await the Council of Chalcedon in A.D. 451 to figure out what this meant. At Chalcedon we learned that Christ has two natures, one human and the other divine, Very God and Very man. This meant that he was as much God as he was man. This was a nonnegotiable claim for the bishops at Chalcedon and became a permanent basic presupposition of the church.

It is therefore not surprising, says Grant, that fifteen centuries later Karl Barth could state, "That God's son or word the man Jesus of Nazareth is the one christological thesis of the New Testament; that the man Jesus of Nazareth is God's son or word is the other."[2] The Chalcedonian definition, says Grant, seems to be cast in stone. Without this Jesus Christ who is both human and divine, Christianity would have no content. It is this Christ who is both savior and sovereign.

Further, the central event of Christian history is the incarnation. The event clearly stated is that God became a man in Jesus Christ. What must women make of this claim? How may women respond to this claim that everyone must pass through this one male figure in order to be saved? This question forces women to reflect on the social context in which Christology emerged and developed. The question sharply focused is, "What has Christology to do with the status of women in this social context?"

WOMANIST THEOLOGY AND CHRISTOLOGY

It is clear to many people that the worldview in which orthodox theology emerged was characterized by the term *patriarchy*. Patriarchy is the male domination of women. In a patriarchal world, women are defined from the perspective of men and are always regarded from a secondary and subordinate role. Grant furthers the definition: "Patriarchalism, then, refers to a metaphysical world-view, a mindset, a way of ordering reality which has more often been associated with the male than the female in Western culture. It is a social system maintaining male dominance and privilege based on female submission and marginality."[3] This worldview suffuses the institutions that control and affect our lives: the military, industry, the university, the church, politics, all areas in which power is institutionalized in society. This means that in a patriarchal system the lives of women are controlled and contained, so that through socialization, they come to accept themselves as secondary and subordinate to men, claims Professor Grant.

It is in this context that theology and Christology emerged and developed. In this worldview, the male is projected as the valued and the female as the devalued entity. At the core of patriarchy is a dualistic view of the world. For example, we talk about self and world, the hierarchical understanding of society, the relation of humanity and nature, and of God and creation: these relationships are modeled on sexual dualism. So to press for the liberation of women is to challenge these stereotypes of authority, identity, and the structural relation of reality. In a male-dominated world, it is easy to understand why God is always thought of as male. This God is the creator and the ruler of the world; while man in turn rules woman, who is beneath him; and she in turn rules the children who are beneath her. According to Grant, this seems to be the theological significance of 1 Cor. 11:3: "But I want you to understand that Christ is the head of every man, and the husband is the head of the wife, and God is the head of Christ." Or again in Eph. 5:22–23: "Wives, be subject to your husbands as you are to the Lord. For the husband is the head of the wife just as Christ is the head of the church, the body of which he is the Savior." According to Grant, the church has used many Christological interpretations to undergird the oppression of women in society and in the church. The question with which we began, "What has Jesus Christ to do with the status of women in church and society?" can be answered tentatively at this point. For many people, Jesus Christ provided normative evidence for the legitimation of the oppression of women. In a country that purports to be Christian and perhaps has more churches than any other country on earth, it is not difficult to understand that the perception that Jesus condoned the subordinate status of women makes it imperative for faithful Christians to carry on the example of Jesus.

In the society at large, it is held that women are the weaker sex, psychologically and politically unequipped for leadership roles. According to Professor Grant, this becomes more feared in the church because the church provides theological and historical justification for its arguments against women holding positions of leadershiop. These arguments are used in the church pertaining to the rite of ordination, and even churches that do ordain women use these arguments to provide a glass ceiling beyond which women may not go. In many churches that do ordain women, they are seldom able to go beyond the positions of minister of education or associate pastor. Perhaps it was this logic that made King appoint Ella Baker for a short time as acting director of the Southern Christian Leadership Council, although she was one of the first persons to conceive of the organization as SCLC.

Grant indicates that another argument that is used to keep women in their place is that Jesus chose twelve disciples who were all men. If Jesus intended the church to have women leaders or ministers, the argument goes, he would have chosen women. This argument is often nonnegotiable, says Grant, because the logic is that if you change the sex of the priest/minister, you alter the image of God. Because Jesus was male, his representatives must be male. The pressing question therefore is: When for centuries this image of Christ has been used to oppress women, can a male Jesus save women? Can women look to this Jesus for the source of salvation? Grant answers affirmatively, provided the old question of Jesus, "Who do men say that I am?" is rephrased to read, "Who do women say that I am?" The problem with the old formulation is not that men, white and Black, answered for women but more important that they negated the validity of the experiences of women. Professor

Grant takes this to its logical conclusion and argues that not only is it inappropriate for men to speak for women, but also white women cannot speak for Black women, because white women do not know the experience of Black women. Although white women, like Black women, have internalized the ways of the master class, not only have white women had access to power in ways Black women have not been able to realize, but white women have been a part of the owner class. Historically, Black women have been a part of the property that white women owned. So although Black and white women share the same gender, and at an ontological level have a common human experience, their experiences have been qualitatively different. Black women must speak for themselves and thereby fashion not a feminist theology but a womanist theology.

Katie Cannon in *Black Womanist Ethics* points out that the white woman, although charged with "the responsibility of being the repository of white civilization," was the only one who could guarantee the purity of the white race and also the only one who could give birth to the legitimate heirs of the white man. Although in a patriarchal world she was placed on a pedestal, regarded as a delicate ornament, and herself internalized the value system in a patriarchal world, yet she was able to give vent to her frustration by punishing and subjecting the Black woman to inhuman treatment. In the white woman's house, the Black woman had to perform the menial and tedious tasks, often under the supervision of the white woman, tasks that the white woman did not want to do. Further, the Black woman had to live in the constant fear that her husband and children would be sold away from her and that she would never see them again.[4] Cannon writes: "As a slave, the Black woman was subjected to the threefold penalization of legal servitude, sexual exploitation and racial discrimination."[5] The experiences of the Black woman are different from not only that of the white female but certainly also from that of the Black male.

Grant and Cannon have provided us with some of the reasons why the names of women in the civil rights movement do not come readily to mind as do those of the men who identified with Martin

Luther King Jr. Most students of the civil rights movement are familiar with the names Jessie Jackson, Ralph David Abernathy, Andrew Young, C. T. Vivian, Hosea Williams, James Lawson, and many others. But if asked to name women who were identified with the movement, they stop with Coretta Scott King, the wife of the slain civil rights leader. There is a sense in which women were invisible in the movement. Not that they were not there, because Rosa Parks started the trail that led to the movement. As someone has said, "She sat down so that Martin Luther King, Jr. may stand up." Further, it was the Women's Political Council at Alabama State College, led by Jo Ann Robinson, that got the leaflets out to advertise the bus boycott. Besides, both the jails and freedom rides were crowded with women. Women who had leadership roles in the movement were Dorothy Cotton, the director of the Citizenship Education Program (CEP); Septima Clark, who was director of the workshops of CEP; and Ella Baker, the acting director of SCLC. Commenting on Baker's tenure as acting director, Cone states:

> *Although she served as its "acting director," most of the male preachers were uneasy with her presence because she did not exhibit the "right attitude" [read "submissiveness"?] which they expected from women, an expectation no doubt shaped by the role of women in their churches. Ella Baker's tenure with SCLC was relatively brief (though longer than she expected), largely because of her conflicts with King and others regarding their attitude toward women and their leadership style built around the charisma of one person—Martin Luther King Jr. Baker preferred the group-centered leadership developed by SNCC, whose founding she initiated.*[6]

King's theology of the beloved community certainly had the theological and moral grounding to provide for the treatment of women as equals in leadership capacities. His move to take all oppressed people seriously certainly had this openness toward all oppressed groups. As his theology dialogues with womanist theology, it must come to see that women also represent the fullness of God's image, that in Jesus Christ all of humanity is redeemed. King's theology must come to see that in Christ a new order is established in which Christ is at work setting all people free. This dialogue must assert that Christ has an especial love for those on the margins of society, the woman of Samaria, the Syro-Phoenician woman, and the widows who are among the outcast. This new dialogue must assert that Christ is at work creating the beloved community, in which people are affirmed and celebrated for their presence.

Grant's plea for a womanist theology raises the issue of the particular and the universal in theological discourse. Do we need a Black theology? Is this the direction in which King's work takes us?

WOMANIST THEOLOGY AND BLACK THEOLOGY

It seems clear that Grant's attempt to delineate between a feminist and a womanist theology calls attention to the necessity of a Black theology as the overarching rubric within which womanist theology must emerge and develop. Womanist theology is imperative, she claims, because Black women's experience is radically different from that of white women. This means that Grant's theology is located within the Black community and within the Black church. It is essentially a theology of the Black experience. And although men, Black or white, are not able to plumb the depths of the womanist experience, because it is a Black thing, they are not excluded. Womanist theology is a theology of the Black experience. That is, the Black experience provides the primary data for talk about God, humanity, and the world. Thus, color—which determines where people live, where they go to school, to which church they belong, whom they marry— becomes a critical category in the development and articulation of this theology. So long as the primary datum is that of the Black experience, one ends up with a Black theology. The category blackness is at once a descriptive and a normative term: descriptive in that it gives specificity and sociological concreteness to the brokenness and tragedy of Black life. At this level blackness points in the direction of gender issues in the Black community but does not yet plumb its depths; yet it is no stranger to the unique dimension represented in the womanist experience. So the particular situation of color that determines one's experience provides a starting point for Black theology. In this sense Black theology is ethnocentric in that it comes out of a specific tradition and situation of oppression, as is the case with African or Caribbean theology. In a rather limited sense, biology is destiny in that who we are shapes our theology. Our biological characteristics, our cultural-psychological traits—our Black experience—provide the point of departure for our articulation about God and humanity.

But not only does blackness point to the existential situation out of which this theology emerges, but blackness also shapes the content of this theology. Christ is Black, states these theologians, because Christ has entered into solidarity with the oppressed. He has identified unequivocally with the oppressed. It is of interest to me that at this point Grant does not go a step further and say, "Christ is Woman." She does not do this because she does not seek to change the historical occurrence in Jesus of Nazareth. Perhaps if she were to anchor her Christology more in the Christology from above rather than Christology from below, it would be more promising in this regard. But being true to the Black church tradition, she does not seek, like some feminist theologians, to tamper with the historical revelation manifested in the man Jesus of Nazareth. Grant does not need to tamper with the historical revelation because womanist theology is neither separatist nor exclusionary.

For Black theology, not only is the context Black in terms of the traditions, the color of the skin, gender, and experiences that are unique to Blacks in America, (slavery, Jim Crow laws, to name a few), but the content of liberation is itself Black. The God who is revealed in Jesus Christ is Black. This God takes sides with the poor, the outcast, the downtrodden, those who hunger and thirst for human justice. Those who have a special love for the gospel. Some people refer to Black people in America as having a religious bent, or as being incurably religious. This claim is a witness to the special affinity the oppressed have for the good news. God has a special love for these people. God sides with the poor.

The keen reader will note that the term *blackness* has a double meaning, and I call attention to this specifically for its capacity for dialogue with womanist theology and its implications for an internal critique of the Black experience. Undoubtedly, the way in which womanist theology forges the way ahead for Black theology and any theology that emerges out of King's thought is its insistence that the experience of Black women is unique, and because of this, not only should Black women's experience not be lumped with that of Black men, but Black men do not speak for Black women. Further, the Black church is asked to be aware of the patriarchal worldview, supported by the Bible and the theology of the church, which not only encourages men to speak for women but excludes women from positions of leadership in the church and in society. Womanist theology sensitizes the church to the ingrained biases that work against women in the church and the workplace. It is of first importance for King's theology to be in conversation with womanist theology so that it may open its eyes to these blind spots.

When womanist theology engages feminist theology in conversation, it raises the issue of the place of class analysis in Black theology in particular and in theological discourse in general. Womanist theology argues that although both Black and white women share a similar form of oppression—together they are oppressed by a patriarchal worldview—the Black woman has an added dimension of oppression in American society because the Black woman has historically been the servant of the white woman. This is an important point, because it forces theology to focus on the place of race, gender, and class in theological discourse. It is not only an important move for theological discourse in general but equally so for the Black church and Black theology in particular, which has focused on issues of race and class but not gender. Womanist theology breaks new ground as it confronts the Black church with the centrality of gender issues in its life and theology. On the other hand, Black theology confronts womanist theology with the possibility of an internal critique along the lines of class analysis.

Womanist theology itself raises the issue of class analysis as it brings Black women into conversation with white women and contends that Black women belong to a different race and a different class and therefore have a different experience. Black women historically belong to the servant class. But what womanist theology fails to do is to look within the womanist experience itself and acknowledge that even there the issue of class is problematic in that it raises the question regarding the quality of the experience highlighted.

Precisely at this point Black theology's attempt to talk about the ontological dimension of blackness becomes important, for at least two reasons. On the one hand, it raises the issue that one may be a Black woman and not committed to the issues of womanist theology, and on the other hand, it is possible that even within the Black woman's world there are women who do not know the experience to which Grant alludes. These women are at a different end of the sociological spectrum; that is, although they share the common problems of gender and race, they do not share the same class, and being of a different class within the Black race raises a central problem for womanist theology.

It is here that I believe womanist theology would find a conversation with Black theology fruitful, because Black theology points out that skin color and gender participation are not enough for womanist theology to become the means for the liberation of all Black women. Commitment to and solidarity with the servant class are important if liberation and reconciliation are to become worthy goals. But another question arises, if the dialogue with Black theology is to prove fruitful: What is the role of not only the particular in theological discourse but also the universal? In what sense, if any, does womanist theology reflect an ontological experience? Granted its uniqueness, that one has to be a Black woman of a particular class to know this experience, which provides a basis for womanist theology, how does one move from the particular to the universal, allowing the womanist experience to become a window through which all people can get vistas of what it means to be truly human? On one level, the question we began with—Can women be saved through Jesus Christ?—is reversed. We ask: Can the experience of women provide a prism through which men can be saved? And we raise a fundamental question: If salvation must come through the womanist experience, can men be saved?

At this precise point Black womanist theology in particular and Black theology in general would benefit from a dialogue with Martin King about the beloved community. Martin King forces the difficult question, In what way is womanist theology Christian theology?¡ Katie Cannon makes the connection, reminding us that King's understanding of the *imago dei* is an appropriate place to begin in that all people, irrespective of social class or racial or ethnic origin, have equal worth because "etched in their personality is the indelible stamp of their creator." Cannon writes: "If Christians believe that God created all people in God's own image and that each person has equal value and worth, then the deliberate injury of another person is morally unjustifiable."[7]

This attempt to relate the one and the many, the particular and the universal, becomes instructive for womanist theology. The dialogue with King opens up the possibility for womanist theology to move from the particular to the universal. Cannon puts it this way: "For Martin Luther King, all of life is interrelated, 'an inescapable network of mutuality,' wherein love serves as the binding force. Agapic love gives natural human relations divine significance and value."[8] For King, this agapic love is at the very center of his thought, and the essential quality of this love is that it is disinterested. This love does not discriminate between worthy and unworthy persons (servant class and employer class, upper class and lower class). This love regards persons as ends and never as means.

Cannon reminds us that there are two related issues that spring forth from this agapic love for King, justice and community. Justice, for King, is more than the absence of strife and discord but signals the presence of human rights being accorded to all of God's children on the basis of their sanctity as inheritors of the *imago dei*. On the other hand, justice points to the human struggle to achieve these rights for all of God's children. This struggle for justice shapes the social and political character of freedom. It may be the right to vote; or access to public accommodations, employment, and health care; or the right to food; or freedom from patriarchal oppression, but struggle is always the form of justice. The expressive force of love and justice has as its goal the creation of the beloved community. It is in this community that womanist theology along with Black theology finds full flowering and expression. Cannon points to the new direction that a conversation with King would take womanist theology:

> *As members of the "beloved community," Black women are responsible, along with others who care, for collecting the facts to determine whether injustice exists, whether a law, an historical situation, existing social relations elevate or debase human beingness. Moral agents must evaluate every situation as to whether it contributes to or impedes the growth of human personality and genuine community. Their task is to determine whether inalienable rights are granted or denied. Ethical living requires an intolerance of civil arrangements that result in the horrors of racism, gender discrimination, economic exploitation and widespread cruelty. The interdependency of the "beloved community" projects a constructive equality of oneness. "Whatever affects one directly affects all indirectly."* [9]

According to Cannon, Black women by themselves do not constitute the "beloved community." She is too faithful to King and the Black church to make that claim, but with the spirit of King, she would state that Black women along with all who care enough about agapic love and justice are willing to struggle for the emergence of "the beloved community."

As we face the twenty-first century, we must press for the renewal of the Church from within, so that it will more closely approximate the new vision of the beloved community. We hope the church will be willing to build on the legacy that King left us— willing to go even further than King and affirm the Black community as the point of departure for talk about God, humanity, and the world. This will become possible because of the peculiar role of Black women, who have always practiced love and signaled a new future for all of God's children. See Black women in many white homes in America raising white children and practicing agapaic love, or see them in their own homes loving their children, their husbands, and fathers and modeling for us the beloved community. The role of Black women in the church and society so closely approximates the African understanding of community that if we are to go forward into a new future, it is wise for us to look to the roots of their understanding of community.

THE ROOTS OF THE BELOVED COMMUNITY

Although King traveled to Africa several times, he did not put his formulation of the "beloved community" in dialogue with an African understanding of community. As the Black church plans for the future, it is instructive for the church to look to African roots for renewal, because that community provided for Black people the context with which the possibility to become more fully human in history became real. Thus, tremendous damage was done to the personality of the Black person when he or she was forced to live outside the indigenous community. Freedom meant a situation in which the self experienced itself in harmony with the community. It was in the context of the community that the self experienced the unity of freedom and destiny. With this understanding of being-in-community one ceased to experience a brother or a sister as the limit to one's freedom but, rather, as the possibility through which the search for identity and meaning was more fully realized. "Existence-in-relation sums up the pattern of the African way of life," Swailem Sidhom says. And this means "a vital link with nature, God, the deities, ancestors, the tribe, the clan, the extended family and himself."[1]

The first man and the first woman, in African traditional religion, were God's people, created by God. In the community they became persons. There the individual discovers himself or herself in

173

terms of duties, privileges, and responsibilities to self and peers. Suffering and joy have meaning only in the community. In marriage neither the wife nor the children "belong" to the nuclear family but to the corporate whole. "Whatever happens to the individual happens to the whole group, and whatever happens to the whole group happens to the individual," writes John Mbiti. "The individual can only say: 'I am, because we are; and since we are therefore I am.' This is the cardinal point in the African view of man."[2]

Because this profound sense of community characterizes African life, the various states of birth, adolescence, marriage, and death are communal events. At birth a child is given three names. The mother's family, the father's family, and the medicine man have the privilege of naming the child. The role of the medicine man is unique, because in a real sense he represents the ancestors, in that it is his task to divine which ancestor entered the child and to name the child accordingly. After the naming of the child, the families celebrate together in a sacrificial feast in which the ancestors are included by the blood of an animal offered as an oblation given to them. In this rite, the parents of the child and the ancestors are united in one community.[3]

An important feature of this corporate relationship is the demand of the individual to engage in a lifestyle that will enhance the well-being of the community. One way to achieve this is for the individual to fulfill his or her destiny in the context of the community. The Yoruba speak of this concept as *Ori,* the Ibo as *Chi,* and the Akan as *Nkraba.* In each instance the destiny is believed to come from God.[4] For the Yoruba, either this destiny of the individual is chosen by the person, or if the person refuses the privilege of free choice, it is assigned by Olodumare, the Supreme Being. According to the Akan, at birth the child enters the world with a purpose. In both cases, there is a sense of compulsion with which one faces the task of fulfilling one's destiny in the community. If one fails to fulfill his or her destiny, the person must return through reincarnation to do so.

People's life in the community is governed not only by social sanctions but by God, who is after all their creator. No one can presume to usurp God's role in dealing with others. Because the neighbor belongs to God, one is never free to hurt the person: "If a man feels aggrieved and disposed to take revenge, he must first seek permission of God. So the Mende of Sierra Leone always invoke the name of God before uttering a curse on anybody."[5] Good or evil can come to a person only in the context of providence. When a person is successful in life, it is thought that the success was made possible because God protects the person. God is "at the person's back." The imagery here is that of the strong protecting the weak. If one escapes danger, it is because God defends him or her; and even if a person commits a crime and is not caught, it is because God is defending and protecting the person: "So the offended party is often heard to exclaim, "O God, do not go on defending and protecting him!"[6] Both good and evil come from God, either directly or indirectly.

Robert Hood assures us in *Must God Remain Greek?* that African religion has shaped the worldview that is pervasive in the socialization and formation of Africans, whether they are Christians, non-Christians, or traditionalists. According to him, even Africans who have abandoned the worldview of their fathers and mothers are still children of their culture. Africans do not forsake their culture. To be cut off from their traditions, community and culture would mean a life of alienation for Africans at home and in the diaspora.

Delores Williams indicates for us the way in which Alice Walker's *In Search of Our Mother's Gardens* makes the connection between womanist thought and Black roots, in history, religion, and culture. Williams writes:

> *The concept womanist allows women to claim their roots in black history, religion and culture. What then is womanist? Her origins are in the black folk expression "You acting womanish," meaning, according to Walker, "wanting to know more and in greater depth than is good for one . . . outrageous, audacious, courageous, and willful behavior." A*

womanist is also "responsible, in charge, serious." She can walk to Canada and take others with her. She loves, she is committed, she is a universalist by temperament. Her universality includes loving men and women, sexually or nonsexually. She loves music, dance, the spirit, food and roundness, struggle, and she loves herself." Regardless."[7]

The anchoring of womanist thought in African roots and its openness to the future and the world may provide clues for the church in its journey forward. According to Alice Walker, the womanist is a universalist, she loves all people, and she loves herself. "Regardless." She is committed to survival and wholeness. She is no separatist.

The vision for the renewal of the church is clear. The church is called to love all people. "Regardless." The church is called to be committed to the wholeness of all people, both women and men. The time to be separate is long past. The new vision would sensitize our consciousness to the need of women for liberation both in their private and public lives. This new vision would build on the work of Martin Luther King Jr.; it would include womanist thought and articulate a new social order that would deal with the complexities of the world in which we live. This vision would include the third world; it would analyze world poverty and sickness, the distribution of this world resources, racism, and sexism. We are told that each day about fifty thousand persons die of hunger and malnutrition— mainly people of color. This new vision must ask what it means to be responsible to the least of these. Within the church we must recall that these are sisters and brothers for whom Christ died.

The way forward is a new social order that presses for the transformation of values both within and without the church. As we press for the renewal of the church, we must pray for and work for new images of wholeness. Womanist theology has helped us to see that in the past, wholeness has been defined in terms of maleness. Within the church, men should not define themselves in relation to the subjugation of women. We must press for new images that spell wholeness for women and men.

Further, this new vision must push for the questioning of institutions that circumscribe the rights of many of God's children. We must teach that the gospel of love demands that our church, our schools, civic organizations, and social groups are to become settings in which all of God's people are free to grow.

In conversation with the third world, this new vision must insist on a redistribution of wealth and power. Basic human rights such as the right to shelter, health care, food, work, education, and play must be secured for all God's people. This new order must be global, involving third world people in a community in which justice, love, forgiveness, kindness, empowerment, and integrity find full expression. This vision must be rooted in the grace of God and in the hopes and dreams of the least of these.

NOTES

FOREWORD

1. Martin Luther King Jr., *Stride Toward Freedom* (San Francisco: Harper & Row, 1986), 224.

1. THE BLACK CHURCH AND KING'S THEOLOGY

1. See "King's Continuing Impact," *Christian Century* 90, no. 2 (10 January 1973): 35–36.

2. Ibid., 36.

3. Herbert Warren Richardson, "Martin Luther King—Unsung Theologian," *Commonweal,* 3 May 1968, 201.

4. James Earl Massey, "The Dream of Community," *The Princeton Seminary Bulletin* 3, no. 9 (1988): 215.

5. James H. Cone, *Black Theology and Black Power* (New York: Seabury Press, 1969), 77–78.

6. See James H. Cone, "Martin Luther King, Jr.: Black Theology— Black Church," *Theology Today* 40 (June 1984): 410.

7. James H. Evans, "Keepers of the Dream: The Black Church and Martin Luther King, Jr.," *American Baptist Quarterly* 5 (March 1986): 82.

8. See Cone, "Martin Luther King: Black Theology—Black Church," 412.

9. Martin Luther King Jr., *Stride Toward Freedom* (San Francisco: Harper & Row, 1986), 84.

10. Ibid., 93–94.

11. King, "Where Do We Go from Here?" in *A Testament of Hope: The Essential Writings of Martin Luther King, Jr.,* ed. James M. Washington (San Francisco: Harper & Row, 1986), 251.

12. E. Franklin Frazier, *The Negro Church in America* (New York: Shocken Books, 1963), 49.

13. King, *Stride Toward Freedom,* 160.

14. Lawrence N. Jones, "The Black Churches: A New Agenda?" *Christian Century* 96, no. 14 (18 April 1979): 434.

15. King, *Why We Can't Wait* (New York: New American Library, 1963), 82–83.

2. PAUL TILLICH'S PERSPECTIVE

1. Paul Tillich, *Systematic Theology* (Chicago: University of Chicago Press, 1967), 89

2. Ibid., 1:60–61.

3. Tillich, "The Problem of Theological Method," *Journal of Religion* 27 (1947): 17.

4. Ibid., 7–8

5. Ibid., 18.

6. Ibid., 20.

7. Ibid.

8. Ibid.

9. Ibid., 22.

10. Ibid.

11. Ibid., 23.

12. Tillich, *Systematic Theology,* 1:171.

13. Ibid.

14. Ibid., 176.

15. See ibid., 179.

16. Ibid., 180.

17. Ibid., 182–83.

18. Ibid., 184–85.

19. Tillich, *The Shaking of the Foundations* (New York: Charles Scribner's Sons, 1955), 57.

20. Tillich, *Systematic Theology,* 1:248.

21. Ibid., 248.

22. Ibid., 249.

23. Ibid., 253–54.

24. Tillich, "Existentialist Thought and Contemporary Philosophy in the West," *Journal of Philosophy* 53, no. 23 (1956): 744.

25. Tillich, *Systematic Theology,* 1:188–89.

26. Ibid., 262.

27. Ibid., 256.

28. Ibid., 266.

29. Ibid., 276.

30. Ibid., 278.

31. Ibid., 282.

32. Ibid., 49.

33. Ibid., 204.

34. Tillich, *Systematic Theology* (Chicago: University of Chicago Press, 1957), 2:99.

35. Tillich, "The Problem of Theological Method," 21.

36. Tillich, *Biblical Religion and the Search for Ultimate Reality* (Chicago: University of Chicago Press, 1955), 38. For a further discussion of this perspective see Tillich, *Systematic Theology,* 1:150–51.

37. Tillich, *Systematic Theology,* 2:59–60.

38. Ibid., 63.

39. Tillich, *World Situation* (Chicago: University of Chicago Press, 1965), 44.

40. Tillich, "The Relevance of the Ministry in Our Time and Its Theological Foundation," in *Making The Ministry Relevant,* ed. Hans Hofmann (New York: Charles Scribner's Sons, 1960), 59–60.

41. Ibid., 32.

42. See Paul Tillich, "Man and Society in Religious Socialism," in *Christianity and Society* 8, no.4 (Fall 1943): 1021. See also Paul Tillich, *The Socialist Decision* (New York: Harper & Row, 1977). For further discussion of Tillich's so-called socialist years, see Wilhelm and Marion Pauck, *Paul Tillich: His Life and Thought* (New York: Harper & Row, 1976), 1:67–79. See also Paul Tillich, *Political Expectation,* ed. James Luther Adams (New York: Harper & Row, 1971).

43. Cited in John J. Ansbro, *Martin Luther King, Jr.: The Making of a Mind* (Maryknoll, N.Y.: Orbis Books, 1982), 60–61.

44. William D. Watley, *Roots of Resistance* (Valley Forge, Pa.: Judson Press, 1985), 42.

45. David J. Garrow, *The FBI and Martin Luther King, Jr.* (New York: Penguin Books, 1981), 218.

3. KARL BARTH'S PERSPECTIVE

1. See Karl Barth, *Revolutionary Theology in the Making,* trans. James D. Smart (Richmond: John Knox Press, 1964), 45.

2. Karl Barth, *The Epistle to the Romans,* trans. Edwyn Hoskins (London: Oxford University Press, 1933), 426–27.

3. Barth, *Revolutionary Theology in the Making,* 28.

4. Hans Urs von Balthasar, *The Theology of Karl Barth* (New York: Doubleday, 1972), 54–55.

5. Barth, *Church Dogmatics,* vol. 1, part 1 (Edinburgh: T & T Clark, 1969), 3.

6. Von Balthasar, *The Theology of Karl Barth,* 77.

7. Barth, *Church Dogmatics,* vol. 1, part 1, 18.

8. Ibid., 10.

9. Ibid., 45.

10. Ibid., 57.

11. Ibid., 115.

12. Ibid., 134.

13. Ibid., 136.

14. Ibid., 343.

15. Ibid., 363.

16. Ibid., 381.

17. Barth, *Evangelical Theology* (Grand Rapids, Mich.: William B. Eerdmans Publishing Co., 1963), ix.

18. Martin Luther King Jr., *Strength to Love* (Cleveland: Collins Publishing Co., 1963), 149. In the essay "Pilgrimage to Nonviolence," King is in dialogue with Tillich, although he does not mention him by name.

19. King, *Strength to Love,* 140–41. In the essay "Paul's Letter to American Christians," King reminds us of the early Barth, or for that matter the early Tillich, while both were avowed socialists. David J. Garrow, in *Bearing the Cross* (New York: William Morrow, 1986), 537, suggests that King was a socialist who chafed at the notion that every time he critiqued the American economic system he was expected to mention that America had to move towards democratic socialism.

20. King, "Pilgrimage to Nonviolence," *Stride Toward Freedom* (San Francisco: Harper & Row, 1958), 99.

21. See King, "Pilgrimage to Nonviolence," *Strength to Love,* 148.

22. See King, "Karl Barth's Conception of God." 2 January 1951, unpublished paper, Archives of the Martin Luther King Jr. Center for Nonviolent Social Change, Atlanta, Ga.

23. Ibid., 2.

24. Ibid., 6.

25. Ibid., 7.

26. Ibid., 9.

4. JAMES CONE'S PERSPECTIVE

1. James H. Cone, *A Black Theology of Liberation* (Philadelphia: J. B. Lippincott, 1970), 197.

2. Ibid., 47–48. The reader will note that the book as a whole illustrates Cone's attempt to relate Barth's and Tillich's approaches to the Black religious experience.

3. James Cone, *Black Theology and Black Power* (New York: Seabury Press, 1969), 112.

4. Ibid., 96.

5. James Cone, *God of the Oppressed* (New York: The Seabury Press, 1975), 5.

6. James Cone, *Black Theology and Black Power*, 83.

7. Ibid., 71.

8. Cecil Wayne Cone, *The Identity Crisis in Black Theology* (Nashville: AMEC Press, 1975), 93.

9. James Cone, *Black Theology and Black Power*, 151.

10. See James H. Cone, "Black Power, Black Theology, and the Study of Theology and Ethics," *Theological Education* 6, no. 3 (Spring 1970): 213.

11. Gayraud Wilmore, *Black Religion and Black Radicalism* (Garden City & New York: Doubleday, 1972), 296.

12. James Cone, *A Black Theology of Liberation* (Philadelphia: J. B. Lippincott, 1970), 23.

13. Ibid., 32.

14. James Cone, *God of the Oppressed*, 1.

15. Ibid., 2.

16. Ibid., 11.

17. James Cone, *My Soul Looks Back* (Maryknoll, N.Y.: Orbis Books, 1986), 65.

18. James Cone, *Black Theology and Black Power*, 96.

19. Ibid., 96–97.

20. Ibid., 108.

21. Ibid., 109.

22. James Cone, *My Soul Looks Back*, 80–81.

23. Ibid., 82.

24. James Cone, *A Black Theology of Liberation*, 30.

25. James Cone, *Black Theology and Black Power*, 69.

26. Ibid., 68.

27. James Cone, *A Black Theology of Liberation*, 198–99.

28. James Cone, *God of the Oppressed*, 108–9.

29. James Cone, *A Black Theology of Liberation*, 202–3.

30. James Cone, *God of the Oppressed*, 117.

31. Ibid., 119–20.

32. Ibid., 121.

33. Ibid., 121.

34. James Cone, *A Black Theology of Liberation,* 231.

35. Ibid., 230.

36. Martin Luther King Jr., *Beyond Vietnam* (New York: Clergy and Laity Concerned, 1967), 2.

37. James Cone, *A Black Theology of Liberation,* 222.

38. James Cone, *God of the Oppressed,* 127.

39. Ibid., 141.

40. Ibid., 110.

41. James Cone, *Black Theology and Black Power,* 40.

42. James Cone, *God of the Oppressed,* 42–43.

43. See James Cone, "Black Theology and the Black Church: Where Do We Go from Here?" in *Black Theology: A Documentary History, 1966–1979,* ed. Gayraud S. Wilmore and James H. Cone (Maryknoll, N.Y.: Orbis Books, 1979), 358.

44. Ibid., 353.

45. Ibid., 356.

46. James Cone, *For My People* (Maryknoll, N.Y.: Orbis Books, 1984), 189–90.

47. Ibid., 195.

48. Ibid., 197.

49. See Cone, "Black Power, Black Theology," 202–15.

50. Ibid., 202.

51. Ibid., 203.

52. Ibid., 206.

53. Ibid., 207.

54. Ibid., 209.

55. Ibid., 211.

56. Ibid., 212.

57. Ibid., 214.

58. James Cone, *God of the Oppressed,* 196–97.

59. Ibid., 198.

60. Ibid., 207.

61. Ibid., 208.

62. Ibid., 214.

63. Cited in ibid., 215–16.

64. Ibid., 218.

65. King, *Beyond Vietnam,* 8–9.

5. MARTIN LUTHER KING JR.'S THEOLOGICAL PERSPECTIVE

1. Martin Luther King Jr., *Why We Can't Wait* (New York: New American Library, 1963), 77, 80.

2. Ibid., 86.

3. Martin Luther King Jr., *Beyond Vietnam* (New York: Clergy and Laity Concerned, 1968), 8–9.

4. King, *Strength to Love,* (Cleveland: Collins Publishers, 1963), 110.

5. King, "A Comparison of the Conceptions of God in the Thinking of Paul Tillich and Henry Nelson Wieman," (Ph.D. diss., Boston University, 1955), 308–9.

6. King, *Stride Toward Freedom* (San Francisco: Harper & Row, 1986), 116.

7. Ibid., 116–17.

8. Ibid., 117.

9. Ibid., 84.

10. See Zelia S. Evans, *Dexter Avenue Baptist Church, 1877–1977* (Montgomery: Dexter Avenue Baptist Church, 1978).

11. King, *Strength to Love,* 150.

12. King, *Stride Toward Freedom,* 171–72.

13. Ibid., 171.

14. See Martin Luther King Jr., "The Power of Nonviolence," in *A Testament of Hope: The Essential Writings of Martin Luther King, Jr.,* ed. James M. Washington (San Francisco: Harper & Row, 1986), 12.

15. King, *Strength to Love,* 154.

16. King, "Facing the Challenge of a New Age," *Testament of Hope,* 141.

17. King, "Facing the Challenge of a New Age" in *Testament of Hope,* 140.

18. King, *Stride Toward Freedom,* 69–70.

19. King, "Remaining Awake through a Great Revolution," in *Testament of Hope,* 269.

20. King, *Stride Toward Freedom,* 105–6.

21. Harold DeWolf, "Martin Luther King, Jr., as Theologian," *The Journal of the Interdenominational Theological Center* 6 (Spring 1977): 4.

22. King, *Strength to Love,* 83.

23. Ibid., 82.

24. Ibid., 82–83.

25. King, "Remaining Awake," 275.

26. King, "The Ethical Demands for Integration," in *Testament of Hope,* 120.

27. Ibid. In King's analysis of freedom we see the hand of Paul Tillich. See also Tillich, *Systematic Theology,* vol. 1 (Chicago: University of Chicago Press, 1951), 184.

28. Ibid., 122.

29. Ibid., 118–19.

30. Ibid., 119.

31. Ibid., 123.

32. Ibid., 124.

33. King, *Strength to Love*, 35.

34. King, Nobel Prize acceptance speech, *Testament of Hope*, 226.

35. Ibid.

36. King, "Where Do We Go from Here?" *Testament of Hope*, 247. For a most helpful analysis of King's attempt to relate love, justice, and power, see Preston Williams, "An Analysis of the Conception of Love and Its Influence on Justice in the Thought of Martin Luther King, Jr," *The Journal of Religious Ethics* 18, no. 2 (Fall 1990): 15–31.

37. King, "Where Do We Go from Here?", 246.

38. Ibid., 251.

39. King, "I See the Promised Land," in *Testament of Hope*, 282.

40. Ibid., 283.

41. Ibid.

42. King, *The Trumpet of Conscience* (New York: Harper & Row, 1967), 14.

43. Ibid., 25.

44. Ibid., 8–9.

45. King, *Strength to Love*, 135.

46. King, *Where Do We Go from Here? Chaos or Community* (Boston: Beacon Press, 1968), 186.

47. James H. Cone, *Martin and Malcolm and America: A Dream or a Nightmare* (Maryknoll, N.Y.: Orbis Books, 1991), 273–74.

6. MARTIN LUTHER KING AND WOMANIST THEOLOGY

1. Jacquelyn Grant, *White Women's Christ and Black Women's Jesus* (Atlanta: Scholars Press, 1989), 63–64.

2. Ibid., 66.

3. Ibid., 68.

4. Katie G. Cannon, *Black Womanist Ethics* (Atlanta: Scholars Press, 1988), 38–39.

5. Ibid., 34.

6. James H. Cone, *Martin and Malcolm and America* (Maryknoll, Orbis Books, 1991), 278.

Cannon, *Black Womanist Ethics,* 163.

id., 165.

., 173.

CONCLUSION: THE ROOTS OF THE BELOVED COMMUNITY

1. Swailem Sidhom, "The Theological Estimate of Man," in *Biblical Revelation and African Beliefs,* ed. Kwesi Dickson and Paul Ellingworth (Maryknoll, N.Y.: Orbis Books, 1973), 102.

2. John S. Mbiti, *African Religions and Philosophy* (New York: Doubleday, 1970), 102.

3. Harry Sawyerr, "Salvation viewed from the African situation," in *Presence,* ed. Bethuel A. Kiplagat (Nairobi, Kenya: World Student Christian Federation, 1969), 17.

4. Ibid., 20.

5. Harry Sawyerr, *Creative Evangelism* (London: Lutterworth Press, 1968), 14.

6. Ibid., 15

7. Delores S. Williams, "Womanist Theology: Black Women's Voices," *Christianity and Crisis* 47, no. 3 (2 March 1987): 66.

BIBLIOGRAPHY

Abernathy, Ralph. *And the Walls Came Tumbling Down: Ralph David Abernathy—An Autobiography*. New York: Harper & Row 1989.

Albert, Peter J., and Ronald Hoffman, eds. *We Shall Overcome: Martin Luther King, Jr., and the Black Freedom Struggle*. New York: Da Capo Press, 1993.

Alinsky, Saul. *Rules for Radicals*. New York: Random House, 1971.

Allen, Robert. *Black Awakening in Capitalist America*. Trenton, N.J.: Africa World Press, 1990.

Anderson, James Desmond. *The Ministry of the Laity and the Corporate Culture of the Gathered Church*. Washington, D.C.: Mount Saint Alban, 1984.

Andolsen, Barbara H., and Christine E. Gudorf, eds. *Women's Consciousness, Women's Conscience: A Reader in Feminist Ethics*. San Francisco: Harper & Row, 1985.

Ansbro, John J. *Martin Luther King, Jr.: The Making of a Mind*. Maryknoll, N.Y.: Orbis Books, 1982.

Baer, Hans A. *The Black Spiritual Movement: A Religious Response to Racism*. Knoxville: University of Tennessee Press, 1984.

Baldwin, James. *The Fire Next Time*. New York: Dial Press, 1963.

Baldwin, Lewis V. *There Is a Balm in Gilead: The Cultural Roots of Martin Luther King, Jr.* Minneapolis: Fortress Press, 1991.

Barbour, Floyd B., ed. *The Black Seventies*. Boston: Porter Sargent Publisher, 1970.

Barth, Karl. *Church Dogmatics*. Vol. 1, part 1. Edinburgh: T & T Clark, 1969.

———. *The Epistle to the Romans*. Translated by Edwyn Hoskins. London: Oxford University Press, 1933.

————. *Evangelical Theology*. Grand Rapids, Michigan: William B. Eerdmans Publishing Company, 1963.

————. *The Humanity of God*. Richmond: John Knox Press, 1960.

————. *Protestant Theology in the Nineteenth Century*. Valley Forge, Pa.: Judson Press, 1973.

————. *Revolutionary Theology in the Making*. Translated by James D. Smart. Richmond: John Knox Press, 1964.

————. *The Word of God and the Word of Man*. Translated by Douglas Horton. New York: Harper & Brothers, 1957.

Bayer, Charles H. *A Guide to Liberation Theology for Middle-Class Congregations*. St. Louis: CBP Press, 1986.

Beach, Waldo, and H. Richard Niebuhr, eds. *Christian Ethics*. London: Alfred A. Knopf, 1973.

Bell, Derrick. *And We Are Not Saved: The Elusive Quest for Racial Justice*. New York: Basic Books, 1987.

————. *Faces at the Bottom of the Well: The Permanence of Racism*. New York: Basic Books, 1992.

Bellah, Robert, et al., eds. *Habits of the Heart*. New York: Harper & Row, 1985.

Benne, Robert. *The Ethic of Democratic Capitalism: A Moral Reassessment*. Philadelphia: Fortress Press, 1981.

Bennett, Lerone. *What Manner of Man*. Chicago: Johnson Publishing Co., 1976.

Booth, William D. *The Progressive Story: New Baptist Roots*. St. Paul, Minn.: Brown Press, 1981.

Bowman, John W. *Prophetic Realism and the Gospel: A Preface to Biblical Theology*. Philadelphia: The Westminster Press, 1955.

Bowne, Borden Parker. *Personalism*. Boston: Houghton Mifflin, 1908.

————. *The Principle of Ethics*. New York: Harper & Brothers, 1892.

Branch, Taylor. *Parting the Waters: America during the King Years, 1954–1963*. New York: Simon & Schuster, 1988.

Brightman, Edgar S. *Moral Laws*. New York: Abingdon Press, 1933.

Brisbane, Robert. *The Black Vanguard*. Valley Forge, Pa.: Judson Press, 1970.

Brown, H. Rap. *Die Nigger Die*. New York: Dial Press, 1969.

Bruce, Calvin E., and William R. Jones, eds. *Black Theology II*. London: Associated University Press, 1978.

Burnham, Frederic B., ed. *Postmodern Theology: Christian Faith in a Pluralist World*. San Francisco: Harper & Row, 1989.

Cade, Toni, ed. *The Black Woman*. Ontario, Canada: New American Library, 1970.

Cannon, Katie. *Black Womanist Ethics*. Atlanta: Scholars Press, 1988.

Carmichael, Stokely, and Charles V. Hamilton. *Black Power: The Politics of Liberation in America*. New York: Vintage Books, 1969.

Carson, Clayborne, ed. *Papers of Martin Luther King, Jr.* Vol. 1, *Called to Serve, January 1929–June 1951*. Berkeley: University of California Press, 1992.

Chopp, Rebecca. *The Praxis of Suffering*. Maryknoll, N.Y.: Orbis Books, 1986.

Cone, Cecil. *The Identity Crisis in Black Theology*. Nashville: AMEC Press, 1975.

Cone, James H. *Black Theology and Black Power*. New York: Seabury Press, 1969.

———. *A Black Theology of Liberation*. Philadelphia: J. B. Lippincott, 1970.

———. *For My People*. Maryknoll, N.Y.: Orbis Books, 1984.

———. *God of the Oppressed*. New York: The Seabury Press, 1975.

———. *Martin and Malcolm and America: A Dream or a Nightmare*. Maryknoll, New York: Orbis Books, 1991.

———. *My Soul Looks Back*. Maryknoll, New York: Orbis Books, 1986.

———. "New Roles in the Ministry: A Theological Appraisal." In *Black Theology: A Documentary History, 1966–1979*. Edited by Gayraud Wilmore and James Cone. Maryknoll, N.Y.: Orbis Books, 1979.

Cort, John C. *Christian Socialism*. Maryknoll, N.Y.: Orbis Books, 1988.

Cox, Harvey. *On Not Leaving It to the Snake*. New York: Macmillan, 1967.

Cruse, Harold. *Crisis of the Negro Intellectual: A Historical Analysis of the Failure of Black Leadership*. New York: Quill, 1967, 1984.

Davis, Angela Y. *Women, Culture, and Politics*. New York: Vintage Books, 1990.

———. *Women, Race, and Class*. New York: Vintage Books, 1983.

Donders, Joseph G. *Non-Bourgeoisie Theology: An African Experience of Jesus*. Maryknoll, N.Y.: Orbis Books, 1986.

Downing, Fred. *To See the Promised Land: The Faith Pilgrimage of Martin Luther King, Jr.* Macon, Ga.: Mercer University Press, 1986.

Dubois, W. E. B. *The Souls of Black Folk*. Chicago: A. C. McClurg & Co., 1903.

Dyck, Arthur C. *On Human Care: An Introduction to Christian Ethics*. Nashville: Abingdon Press, 1977.

Ellison, Mary. *The Black Experience: American Blacks since 1865*. New York: Barnes & Noble, 1974.

Ellul, Jacques. *Jesus and Marx: From Gospel to Ideology*. Grand Rapids, Mich.: William B. Eerdmans Publishing Co., 1988.

Elshtain, Jean Bethke. *Public Man, Private Woman: Women in Social and Political Thought*. Princeton: Princeton University Press, 1981.

Evans, Zelia S. *Dexter Avenue Baptist Church, 1877–1977*. Montgomery, Ala.: Dexter Avenue Baptist Church, 1978.

Fackre, Gabriel. *The Religious Right and Christian Faith*. Grand Rapids, Mich.: William B. Eerdmans Publishing Co., 1982.

Fairclough, Adam. *To Redeem the Soul of America: The Southern Christian Leadership Conference and Martin Luther King, Jr.* Athens: University of Georgia Press, 1987.

Farley, Edward. *The Fragility of Knowledge: Theological Education in the Church and the University*. Philadelphia: Fortress Press, 1988.

————. *Theologia: The Fragmentation and Unity of Theological Education*. Philadelphia: Fortress Press, 1983.

Foner, Philip S. ed. *Black Socialist Preacher: The Teachings of Reverend George Washington Woodbey and His Disciple Reverend George W. Slater, Jr.* San Francisco: Synthesis Publications, 1983.

Fordham, Monroe. *Major Themes in Northern Black Religious Thought, 1800–1860*. Hicksville, N.Y.: Exposition Press, 1975.

Forell, George W. *Christian Social Teachings*. Minneapolis: Augsburg Publishing House, 1966.

Fowler, James. *Stages of Faith*. San Francisco: Harper & Row, 1981.

Franklin, Robert M. *Liberating Visions: Human Fulfillment and Social Justice in African-American Thought*. Minneapolis: Fortress Press, 1990.

Frazier, E. Franklin. *Black Bourgeoisie*. New York: Collier Books, 1957.

————. *The Negro Church in America*. New York: Shocken Books, 1963.

Friesen, Duane. *Christian Peacemaking and International Conflict: A Realist Pacifist Perspective*. Scottdale, Pa.: Herald Press, 1986.

Garrow, David. *Bearing the Cross: Martin Luther King, Jr. and the Southern Christian Leadership Conference*. New York: William Morrow, 1986.

————. *The FBI and Martin Luther King, Jr.: From "Solo" to Memphis*. New York: W. W. Norton, 1981. Reprint, New York: Penguin Books, 1981.

Goba, Bonganjalo. *An Agenda for Black Theology: Hermeneutics for Social Change*. Johannesburg, South Africa: Skotaville Publishers, 1988.

Grant, Jacquelyn. *White Women's Christ and Black Women's Jesus*. Atlanta: Scholars Press, 1989.

Gustafson, James. *Ethics from a Theocentric Perspective*. Vol. 2, *Ethics and Theology*. Chicago: University of Chicago Press, 1984.

Gutierrez, Gustavo. *A Theology of Liberation: History, Salvation, and Politics*. Maryknoll, N.Y.: Orbis Books, 1984.

Hacker, Andrew. *Two Nations: Black and White, Separate, Hostile, Unequal*. New York: Charles Scribner's Sons, 1992.

Hampton, Henry, and Steve Fayer. *Voices of Freedom: An Oral History of the Civil Rights Movement from the 1950s through the 1980s*. New York: Bantam Books, 1990.

Handy, Robert T. *The Social Gospel in America, 1870–1920*. New York: Oxford University Press, 1966.

Hanigan, James P. *Martin Luther King, Jr., and the Foundations of Nonviolence*. Latham, Md.: University Press of America, 1984.

Harrington, Michael. *The Other America: Poverty in the United States*. Middlesex, England: Penguin Books, 1981.

Harvey, Van A. *A Handbook of Theological Terms*. New York: Macmillan, 1964.

Hauerwas, Stanley. *Should War Be Eliminated?* Milwaukee: Marquette University Press, 1984.

Hessel, Dieter T., ed. *Theological Education for Social Ministry*. New York: Pilgrim Press, 1988.

Hodgson, Peter C., and Robert H. King, eds. *Christian Theology*. Philadelphia: Fortress Press, 1985.

Hooks, Bell. *Black Looks: Race and Representation*. Boston: South End Press, 1992.

Hooks, Bell, and Cornel West. *Breaking Bread: Insurgent Black Intellectual Life*. Boston: South End Press, 1991.

Howard-Pitney, David. *The Afro-American Jeremiad: Appeals for Justice in America*. Philadelphia: Temple University Press, 1990.

Jaynes, Gerald David and Robin M. Williams, eds. *A Common Destiny: Blacks and American Society*. Washington, D.C.: National Academy Press, 1989.

Kahane, Howard. *Thinking about Basic Beliefs: An Introduction to Philosophy*. Belmont, Ca.: Wadsworth, 1983.

Kant, Immanuel. *Foundations of the Metaphysics of Morals*. Translated by Lewis Beck. New York: Library of Liberal Arts Press, 1959.

King, Coretta Scott. *My Life with Martin Luther King, Jr.* New York: Holt, Rinehart, and Winston, 1969.

———. *The Words of Martin Luther King, Jr.* New York: Newmarket Press, 1983, 1987.

King, Martin Luther, Jr. *The Measure of a Man*. Philadelphia: Fortress Press, 1959.

———. *Strength to Love*. Cleveland: Collins Publishing Co., 1963.

————. *Stride Toward Freedom*. San Francisco: Harper & Row, 1986.

————. *A Testament of Hope: The Essential Writings of Martin Luther King, Jr.* Edited by James M. Washington. San Francisco: Harper & Row, 1986.

————. *The Trumpet of Conscience*. New York: Harper & Row, 1967.

————. *Where Do We Go from Here? Chaos or Community* Boston: Beacon Press, 1967.

————. *Why We Can't Wait*. New York: New American Library, 1963.

King, Paul G., and Kent Maynard. *Risking Liberation: Middle Class Powerlessness and Social Heroism*. Atlanta: John Knox Press, 1988.

Knudson, Albert C. *The Principles of Christian Ethics*. New York: Abingdon Press, 1943.

LeFevre, Perry, ed. *Man: Six Modern Interpretations*. Philadelphia: Geneva Press, 1966.

Leith, John. *John Calvin's Doctrine of the Christian Life*. Louisville: Westminster/John Knox Press, 1989.

Lincoln, C. Eric, ed. *The Black Experience in Religion*. New York: Doubleday, 1974.

————. *Martin Luther King, Jr.: A Profile*. New York: Hill & Wang, 1970.

————. *Race, Religion, and the Continuing American Dilemma*. New York: Hill & Wang, 1984.

Lokos, Lionel L. *A House Divided: The Life and Legacy of Martin Luther King*. New Rochelle, N.Y.: Arlington House, 1968.

Lundin, Roger: *The Culture of Interpretation: Christian Faith and the Postmodern World*. Grand Rapids, Mich.: William B. Eerdmans Publishing Company, 1993.

McClendon, James W. *Biography as Theology*. Nashville: Abingdon, 1974.

McGovern, Arthur F. *Marxism: An American Christian Perspective*. New York: Orbis Books, 1987.

Mappes, Thomas A., and Jane S. Zembaty. *Social Ethics: Morality and Social Policy*. New York: McGraw-Hill, 1987.

Marable, Manning. *How Capitalism Underdeveloped Black America: Problems in Race, Political Economy, and Society*. Boston: South End Press, 1983.

————. *Race, Reform, and Rebellion: The Second Reconstruction in Black America, 1945–1982*. Jackson: University Press of Mississppi, 1984.

Mbiti, John S. *African Religions and Philosophy*, New York: Doubleday, 1970.

Metz, Johannes B. *The Emergent Church*. New York: Crossroad Publishing Co., 1981.

——. *Faith in History and Society.* New York: Seabury Press, 1980.

——. *Theology of the World.* New York: Seabury Press, 1969.

Midgely, Mary, and Judith Hughes. *Women's Choices: Philosophical Problems Facing Feminism.* New York: St. Martin's Press, 1983.

Miller, Keith D. *Voice of Deliverance: The Language of Martin Luther King, Jr., and Its Sources.* New York: Free Press, 1992.

Mitchell, Henry. *Black Belief.* New York: Harper & Row, 1975.

Moltmann, Jurgen. *The Crucified God.* New York: Harper & Row, 1974.

——. *On Human Dignity: Political Theology and Ethics.* Philadelphia: Fortress Press, 1977.

Moraga, Cherrie, and Gloria Anzaldua, eds. *The Bridge Called My Back: Writings by Radical Women of Color.* Watertown, Mass: Persephone Press, 1981.

Morris, Aldon. *Origins of the Civil Rights Movement.* New York: Free Press, 1984.

Namorato, Michael V., ed. *Have We Overcome?* Jackson: University Press of Mississippi, 1979.

Nash, Arnold, ed. *Protestant Thought in the Twentieth Century.* New York: Macmillan, 1951.

Newbigin, Leslie. *Truth to Tell: The Gospel and Public Truth.* New York: William B. Eerdmans, 1991.

Niebuhr, H. Richard. *Christ and Culture.* New York: Harper & Row, 1951.

Oates, Stephen. *Let the Trumpet Sound.* New York: Harper & Row, 1982.

Paglia, Camille. *Sex, Art, and American Culture.* New York: Vintage Books, 1992.

——. *Sexual Personae: Art and Decadence From Nefertiti to Emily Dickinson.* New York: Vintage Books, 1990.

Paris, Peter. *Black Religious Leaders: Conflict in Unity.* Louisville: Westminster/John Knox Press, 1991.

——. *Social Teachings of the Black Churches.* Philadelphia: Fortress Press, 1985.

Pauck, Wilhelm and Marion. *Paul Tillich: His Life and Thought.* Vol. 1. New York: Harper & Row, 1976.

Phillips, Kevin. *The Politics of Rich and Poor: Wealth and the American Electorate in the Reagan Aftermath.* New York: Random House, 1990.

Rauschenbusch, Walter. *Christianity and the Social Crisis.* New York: Harper & Row, 1907.

——. *A Theology for the Social Gospel.* New York: Macmillan, 1917.

Reddick, Lawrence. *Crusader without Violence: A Biography of Martin Luther King, Jr.* New York: Harper & Brothers, 1959.

Reist, Benjamin. *Toward a Theology of Involvement: The Thought of Ernst Troeltsch.* Philadelphia: Westminster Press, 1966.

Runyon, Theodore. "Tillich's Understanding of Revolution." In *Theonomy and Autonomy.* Edited by John Carey. Atlanta: Mercer University Press, 1984.

Sawyerr, Harry. *Creative Evangelism.* London: Lutterworth Press, 1968.

Scott, Robert L., and Wayne Brockriede, eds. *The Rhetoric of Black Power.* New York: Harper & Row, 1969.

Soelle, Dorothy. *Suffering.* Philadelphia: Fortress Press, 1975.

Sowell, Thomas. *A Conflict of Visions: Ideological Origins of Political Struggles.* New York: William Morrow, 1987.

Stackhouse, Max. *Public Theology and Political Economy.* New York: University Press of America, 1991.

Stang, Alan. *It's Very Simple—The True Story of Civil Rights.* Belmont: Western Islands Publishers, 1965.

Stringfellow, William. *Dissenter in a Great Society.* New York: Holt, Rinehart, & Winston, 1966.

Taylor, Kline Mark. *Paul Tillich: Theologian of the Boundaries.* San Francisco: Collins Liturgical Publications. 1987.

Terkel, Studs. *Race: How Blacks and Whites Think and Feel about the American Obsession.* New York: The New Press, 1992.

Tillich, Paul. *Biblical Religion and the Search for Ultimate Reality.* Chicago: The University of Chicago Press, 1955.

———. *Love, Power, and Justice.* London: Oxford University Press, 1954.

———. *Political Expectation.* Edited by James Luther Adams. New York: Harper & Row, 1971.

———. *The Religious Situation.* Translated by H. Richard Niebuhr. New York: H. Holt, 1932.

———. *The Shaking of the Foundations.* New York: Charles Scribner's Sons, 1955.

———. *The Socialist Decision.* New York: Harper & Row, 1977.

———. *Systematic Theology.* Vol. 1. Chicago: University of Chicago Press, 1967.

———. *Systematic Theology.* Vol. 2, *Existence and the Christ.* Chicago: The University of Chicago Press, 1957.

———. *Theology of Culture.* London: Oxford University Press, 1964.

———. *World Situation.* Chicago: The University of Chicago Press, 1965.

Tracy, David. *The Analogical Imagination: Christian Theology and the Culture of Pluralism.* New York: Crossroads Press, 1981.

Turner, Jonathan H. *Patterns of Social Organization.* New York: McGraw-Hill, 1972.

van Dijk, Tuen A. *Communication Racism: Ethnic Prejudice in Thought and Talk.* Newbury Park, Calif.: Sage Publications, 1987.

von Balthasar, Hans Urs. *The Theology of Karl Barth.* New York: Doubleday, 1972.

Walker, Theodore. *Empower the People: Social Ethics for the African-American Church.* Maryknoll, N.Y.: Orbis Books, 1991.

Walton, Hanes. *The Political Philosophy of Martin Luther King, Jr.* Westport, Conn.: Greenwood, 1971.

Washington, James M. *Frustrated Fellowships: The Black Baptist Quest for Social Power.* Macon: Mercer University Press, 1986.

Washington, Joseph R. *Black Religion.* Boston: Beacon Press, 1964.

————. *Black Sects and Cults.* Garden City, N.Y.: Doubleday: 1973.

———— *The Politics of God.* Boston: Beacon Press, 1967.

Washington, Joseph. ed. *Black Religion and Public Policy.* Philadelphia: University of Pennsylvania Press, 1978.

Watley, William D. *Roots of Resistance.* Valley Forge, Pa.: Judson Press, 1985.

West, Cornel. *Prophetic Fragments.* Grand Rapids, Mich.: William B. Eerdmans, 1988.

————. *Race Matters.* Boston: Beacon Press, 1993.

Wilmore, Gayraud. *Black Religion and Black Radicalism.* Garden City, N.Y.: Doubleday, 1972. Reprint, Maryknoll, N.Y.: Orbis Books, 1984.

Wilson, William J. *The Declining Significance of Race: Blacks and Changing American Institutions.* 2d ed. Chicago: University of Chicago Press, 1980.

———— . *The Truly Disadvantaged: The Inner City, the Underclass, and Public Policy.* Chicago: University of Chicago Press, 1987.

Wolfenstein, Eugene Victor. *The Victims of Democracy: Malcolm X and the Black Revolution.* New York: The Guilford Press, 1993.

Wright, Anthony. *Socialisms: Theories and Practices.* New York: Oxford University Press, 1986.

Young, Alfred F., ed. *Dissent.* DeKalb: Northern Illinois University Press, 1968.

Zepp, Ira, and Kenneth Smith. *Search for the Beloved Community: The Thinking of Martin Luther King, Jr.* Valley Forge, Pa.: Judson Press, 1974.

INDEX

Foreman, James, Black manifesto
of, 84–85
form, application to divine life,
25
For My People (Cone), 112
Frazier, E. Franklin, 5, 6–7
Frazier, E. Stanley, 136, 137
freedom: King on, 147–48, 149,
154; meaning of, for Black
community, 173; as ontological,
23–24; Tillich on, 36–37, 147

Gandhi, Mohandâs, 3
Garnet, Highland, 93
Garrow, David, 47
Garvey, Marcus, 84
God: Barth's conception of, 47,
79–80; King's understanding of,
9–10, 141–47; as power of be-
ing, 24–27; Tillich on, 24–31,
45, 135
God of the Oppressed (Cone), 122
Gogarten, Friedrich, 58
Goldstein, K., 28
Good Samaritan, King on, 150,
151
Göttingen, 60
Graham, Billy, 85
Grant, Jacquelyn, 159–63, 165–
66, 168

hate, King on, 151
heaven, Cone on meaning of, 107
Hebrews 4:15, 32
Herrmann, Wilhelm, 50
Hitler, Adolf, 86–87
Hood, Robert, 175
hubris, Tillich on, 36
human freedom, Cone on grounding of, 109–10

humanity: King's doctrine of,
147–54; Tillich's doctrine of,
35–38
human nature, Barth on, 79
human situation, Cone on, 91

Ibo, 174
"I-it" relationship, 10, 149
imago dei, 169–70, 170
incarnation: Barth on, 74; King
on, 160
inclusivity, King on, 91
indeterminism, Tillich on, 23
individualization of God, Tillich
on, 21, 25
injustice, King on, 78–79
*In Search of Our Mother's Gar-
dens* (Walker), 175
intentionality, Tillich on, 22–23
Irenaeus, 86
irregular theology, 68–69, 77–78
isness, 102–3
"I-thou" relationship, 10, 149

Jackson, Jesse, 113, 164
Jasper, Karl, 85
Jesus Christ: Barth on, 52–53,
160; Black church on teachings
of, 5; Cone on understanding
historical, 100–101; as faith,
claim, 32–33; as historical fact,
32–34; humanity of, as central
theme of black ecclesiology,
101–2; King on death of, 150–
51; King on gospel of, 137–38,
156; King on life and teaching
of, 2–3; as New Being, 31–34;
and oppression of women, 161–
63; relevance of, for Black
community, 117–18